ADVANCING THROUGH ADVERSITY

CHARLES STANLEY

OLIVER
NELSON

THOMAS NELSON PUBLISHERS
Nashville • Atlanta • London • Vancouver

Published in Nashville, Tennessee, by Thomas Nelson, Inc., Publishers, and distributed in Canada by Word Communications, Ltd., Richmond, British Columbia.

The Bible version used in this publication is THE NEW KING JAMES VERSION. Copyright © 1979, 1980, 1982, Thomas Nelson, Inc., Publishers.

ISBN 0-7852-7258-5

Printed in the United States of America.

3 4 5 6 — 01 00 99 98 97

CONTENTS

GOD HAS A PURPOSE FOR EVERYTHING THAT HAPPENS TO YOU

Adversity has a positive side.

I realize that isn't a statement you are likely to hear very often. Your first response may have been, "Oh, really? You don't know what I'm going through!"

To see the positive side of adversity is not wishful thinking, denial of reality, or pie-in-the-sky optimism. Rather, it is a statement of faith.

The positive side of adversity is rooted in two strong beliefs:

First, God has a plan and a purpose for the life of every person, including you. If you desire for God's plan and purpose to be accomplished in your life, the Lord will go to whatever lengths are necessary to see His plan and purpose fulfilled in your life. He will not go against your will, but if your will is to desire His will, then the Lord will move heaven and earth to see that His will is done in and through you. Believing this means, of course, that God can *use* any adversity that comes your way for His plan, to further your purposes on the earth or to work His purposes within your life.

Second, God can turn things to good for you regardless of the situation you are facing today. You may think your life has derailed and crashed beyond any repair. But the Scriptures say, "We know that all things work together for good to those who love God, to those who are the called according to His purpose" (Rom. 8:28).

The Lord has a way of arranging things so that good comes from bad. That's His very nature as Redeemer—to take what attempts to enslave us and to use it to free us. Not only that, but when the Lord redeems a situation, He also sends a message to other people who observe what God is doing in our lives. That message may bring about many different reactions—from conviction to repentance to praise. What God does for good in our lives is never limited to us; it is always for others, too.

Jesus taught this to His disciples through the healing of a man who was blind in Jerusalem. The disciples asked Jesus after the man had been healed, "Who sinned, this man or his parents, that he was born blind?" (John 9:2). The disciples had been taught all their lives that illness was a sign of God's judgment. They had no doubt whatsoever that somebody had sinned to cause the condition of blindness.

Jesus replied, "Neither this man nor his parents sinned, but that the works of God should be revealed in him" (John 9:3). There was purpose to the man's adversity. The disciples saw his blindness as *being caused by* something bad. Jesus taught that the man's blindness was *for the cause of* something good.

Note that Jesus didn't say, "This man is blind because he sinned, but God is going to use it anyway." That would be a much easier statement for many of us to swallow. Rather, Jesus said that God had a purpose higher than anything the disciples had considered. God intended to use the miracle to bring about something positive and eternal in the man's life and in the lives of people who witnessed his healing.

That puts an entirely new light on any type of adversity we may experience. While there is good reason to be concerned about what causes adversity—which we will deal with later on in this book—

our greater concern must always be with what results from adversity. Do we allow adversity to throw us back, defeat us, or pull us down? Or do we see adversity as something that can make us stronger, better, and more whole?

Do we regard adversity as a destroyer? Or do we see it as having within it the seeds that can produce something beneficial and helpful?

Do we see adversity as linked to death? Or do we see it as linked to growth and eventually to eternal life?

Do we look for the results caused by adversity to be negative or situation bound? Or do we look for the results of adversity to be part of God's miracle-working, for-our-good plan?

This book is concerned with how we can *advance* through adversity. Adversity can be a teacher. From adversity, and especially as we work through adversity by our faith and according to God's Word, we can learn valuable lessons that prepare us fully to be the people God created us to be.

Yes, God has a plan and a purpose for your life.

And yes, God can use whatever comes against your life for your good.

Reflect on these questions as you prepare for this study:

- *How do you perceive adversity?*

  _____

  _____

- *Can you see how God has caused something good to come from an adversity you have experienced?*

  _____

  _____

- *Which has the greater power to determine your future—the situations in which you find yourself (including adversity) or your faith in the Lord Jesus Christ?*

  _____

  _____

ADOPTING A PERSPECTIVE ON ADVERSITY

Much has been written about how to overcome the odds, recover from trouble, and get answers to problems. Bookstores are lined with self-help books. This book you hold in your hands, however, is better labeled a Bible-help book.

When adversity strikes our lives, we eventually reach the end of our ability to help ourselves. Our end point is often God's beginning point. The help that God offers us in His Word—the Bible—is eternal, but it is also timely. My hope is that as you engage in this study, you will find yourself referring to your Bible again and again—to mark specific words or underline phrases.

The Bible is God's foremost communication tool. It is the wellspring of eternal wisdom. It is the reference to which we must return continually to compare what is happening in us and to us to what should be happening in us and what can happen to us.

Make notes in the margins of your Bible as you engage in this study. It is far more important that you write God's insights into your Bible, which you are reading regularly, than to write in this book, although places are provided for you to make notes here.

Keys to Study

You will be asked at various points to identify with the material presented by answering one or more of these questions:

- What new insight have you gained?
- Have you ever had a similar experience?
- How do you feel about this?
- In what way are you challenged to act?

Insights

A spiritual insight occurs when you see something as if it is new. You might have read, studied, analyzed, or meditated on a particular verse many times—even to the point that you think there is nothing else you could possibly learn about the verse. And then, God suddenly reveals new meaning to you. That is a spiritual insight.

Insights are usually very personal, and they usually relate to something you are experiencing or have experienced in your life. Ask God to give you insights every time you open His Word to read it. I believe He'll answer that prayer.

It is important in Bible study to note the insights we receive into God's Word. We are better able to review them later in the light of other Scriptures. We also have them more readily available to share with others. And then, too, most people find that the more they look and listen for insights—in a very intentional, focused way—the more God gives insight.

Periodically in this study, you will be asked to note what specific passages of the Bible say to you. These are places to record insights.

Experiences

Each of us comes to God's Word from a unique background; therefore, each of us has a unique perspective on what is read. Never dismiss the value of life experiences. They are part of the way God teaches us. We have experiences about which we can say, "I know that truth in the Bible is real because of what happened to me." And the more we see the Bible as relating to our personal experiences, the more the Bible confirms, encourages, convicts, challenges, and transforms us. We grow in our understanding that God's Word is universal, as well as individual and personal, and that there isn't anything that we encounter as human beings that isn't addressed by the Bible in one or more ways.

Sharing experiences in your journey of faith is essential for your spiritual growth. Even if you are doing this study on your own, I encourage you to converse with others about your faith experiences. Allow others to learn from you even as you learn from them.

Emotional Response

Just as each of us has unique experiences in life, each of us has unique emotional responses to God's Word. No one emotional response is more valid than another. You may be frightened or perplexed—or feel great joy or relief—at what you read. Another person may have a very different response.

Face your emotions honestly. Learn to share your emotions with others.

Neither experience nor emotions make the Bible true. The Bible is truth, period. Rather, our feelings and experiences can provide evidence of the Bible's truth. What we read in the Bible has an emotional impact on us. Sometimes we are moved to tears by what we read, at other times we may feel great elation, conviction, hope, love, longing, surprise, or a host of other emotions.

I am asking you to recognize that the Scriptures allow you to have an emotional response to them. God created you with emotions. He knows that you feel certain ways toward Him, toward others, and toward His Word. You may find it easier to start doing what the Bible tells you to do after you identify how you feel about what God says to you.

As you meet with others to study adversity and how to advance in your spiritual life during times of adversity, stay focused on what the Bible says. Let the Bible speak for itself. A Bible study often can get sidetracked by opinions registered by the various people in a group. When it comes right down to it, our opinion is of little significance when we study the Bible. It is far more beneficial when we share experiences in which the Bible has come alive for us in our lives, or when we share our feelings about what the Bible says, than when we share what we think about a particular passage. None of us understand the Bible fully—it is a spiritual book that reflects the unfathomable riches of God's Spirit—but each of us has a valid emotional and life experience link to God's Word.

Challenges

As we read the Bible, we need to come to the place where we feel challenged to do something in response to what we have read or studied. God is never content with our status quo. He always wants us to grow more like His Son, Jesus Christ. Real growth comes not in understanding God's Word, but in applying God's Word. A farmer once said to me, "I can understand all the benefits of fertilizer, but it doesn't do my field any good until I apply it to the plants." The Bible challenges us to be doers of His Word and not hearers only (James 1:22).

We need to pinpoint, as best we can, the areas in which we believe God is challenging us, stretching us, or causing us to believe for more. When we say to ourselves, "This is what I believe God wants me to do," we are identifying the next step in our spiritual growth.

Ultimately, God desires to get His Word into us, and us into His Word, so we can share His Word with others. Sometimes we are asked to share His Word with people who don't know the Lord or who have never read the Bible. At other times we are asked to share His Word with people who are fellow Christians and Bible students. The important thing is not with whom we share the Word as much as our willingness to share it with others as often as possible and to be open to the leading of the Lord at all times, fully expecting that He will show us the appropriate times and places to be His witnesses.

If you don't have somebody with whom to discuss your insights, experiences, emotions, and challenges, I encourage you to find somebody. Perhaps you can start a Bible study in your home. Perhaps you can talk to your pastor about organizing Bible study groups in your church. There is much to be learned on your own.

There is much more to be learned as you become part of a small group that desires to grow in the Lord.

Keep the Bible Central

At all times, keep the Bible itself central to your study. Gather around God's Word as if you are gathering around a dinner table—to draw spiritual nourishment from it so that each person who partakes may grow in the Lord.

If you are doing a personal Bible study, be diligent in keeping your focus on God's Word. Self-analysis or personal recovery is not the goal of this study. Growing up into the fullness of the stature of Christ Jesus is the goal!

Prayer

Finally, I encourage you to begin and end your Bible study times in prayer. Ask God to give you spiritual eyes to see what He wants you to see and spiritual ears to hear what He wants you to hear. Ask Him to give you new insights, to remind you of experiences that relate to what you read, and to help you clarify your feelings about what you read. Ask Him to reveal to you what He desires for you to be, say, and do.

As you conclude your time of study, ask the Lord to seal what you have learned to your heart so that you will never forget it. Ask Him to transform you more into the likeness of Jesus Christ as you meditate on what you have studied. And above all, ask Him to give you the courage to become, say, and do what He has challenged you to become, say, and do. Pray for boldness to be faithful to His calling in your life.

Consider these questions:

- *What new insights about how to deal with adversity do you desire to gain from this study?*

_____

_____

- *In what areas have you struggled with the idea of adversity or suffering?*

  _____

  _____

- *How do you feel about the prospect that God may have a purpose for adversity in your life?*

  _____

  _____

- *Are you open to growing in your faith?*

  _____

  _____

THE TWO QUESTIONS WE ASK WHEN ADVERSITY STRIKES

—AND THE ONE QUESTION WE SHOULD ASK

When adversity strikes, we tend to ask two questions almost as an automatic response:

1. Why did this happen?
2. Who is responsible for this?

Subconsciously or consciously, verbally or silently, these questions spring to our minds and lips.

Are they good questions to ask? That's the focus of this lesson.

Why Ask Why?

A popular commercial asks the question, "Why ask why?" In many cases, there are very good reasons to ask *why* in our world today! *Why* is one of the most potent questions any person can ever ask about anything. It is the question at the root of curiosity and discovery—a question that can lead to wonderful insights, creative applications, theories, inventions, and solutions.

When we ask *why* in the face of adversity, however, our question is nearly always couched in highly personal terms: "Why did this happen to me?" The focus is less on *why* and more on *me*.

The more valid perspective, of course, is probably to ask, "Why *not* me?" We live in a fallen world. Sin abounds. The human heart has evil intent. Accidents occur. Nobody is perfect. The devil is real, and the Scriptures tell us that he is continually walking about "like a roaring lion, seeking whom he may devour" (1 Peter 5:8).

The Lord never promised to keep you or any of His children from all adversity or to adjust all circumstances for your exclusive benefit and pleasure. Rather, the Scriptures tell us that the Lord "makes His sun rise on the evil and on the good, and sends rain on the just and on the unjust" (Matt. 5:45). The circumstances of life are just that—the circumstances of life. Problems, needs, and troubles plague all of humankind. No one is immune to them.

We cannot assume that the Lord will keep us free of all adversity and harm, but we can count on the Lord's being with us in times of adversity, calamity, tragedy, hardship, and pain.

Most of us are familiar with Psalm 23:4:

> *Yea, though I walk through the valley of the shadow of death,*
> *I will fear no evil;*
> *For You are with me;*
> *Your rod and Your staff, they comfort me.*

We hear that psalm during funeral services or recall it in times of severe illness or tragedy, but the psalmist does not say the "valley of death"—rather, it's the "valley of the shadow of death." The shadow of death refers to situations and circumstances that may cause us harm, loss, defeat, destruction, discouragement, pain, sorrow, suffering and, ultimately, death itself. Shadows are foreboding and ominous, so even the fear of potential adversity can be included in our interpretation of the "valley of the shadow of death."

Note further, however, that the psalmist's intent is not to instill fear about such a valley but to proclaim, "I will fear no evil; for You are with me." That's the right approach toward adversity.

When adversity hits us, as it surely will at some point in life, we are wise to say, "No matter what I may experience, the Lord is with me. He is walking through this with me. He is right here by my side. He knows the situation, and He knows the way through the situation to a brighter and better tomorrow!"

The better *why* question to ask is, "Why this?" In other words, why did *this* happen as opposed to other things that could happen? There is an explanation—apart from an accusation of faultfinding—for most things that happen to us. A person may lose a house in a mud slide and have to face the fact that he bought a home on the side of a hill in an area prone to mud slides. A person may have a serious illness and learn as a result that she should have made different choices about her health ten or twenty years ago. A couple may face marital difficulties and look back and see where they could have communicated better, given more selflessly, or sought out counseling much earlier in their relationship. A person may be in an automobile accident and learn a great deal about how to improve his life and driving skills.

At other times, the explanation for the adversity may be something that is totally outside a person's control or influence. Even so, an explanation can be beneficial to bringing closure to a situation. A person may experience a loss from a hurricane, flood, or tornado, and the explanation simply may be that he lives in a place where hurricanes, floods, or tornadoes are likely to occur. A person may suffer a financial loss on the stock market, and the explanation is ultimately that stock market investments have risks associated with them, even if she chooses the most reputable and seemingly stable companies in which to invest.

Getting to the foundational reason or the logical explanation for adversity can be beneficial to us because such an explanation can provide valuable information about what not to do in the future. If there is a spiritual root to the adversity, the Lord desires that we face our sinfulness, repent of it (which means literally to change our ways and begin to walk according to God's way), learn from our experience, or have that particular root of evil or problem pulled out of our lives by the healing, cleansing, redeeming power of the Holy Spirit. Yes, we can learn from adversity and, in so doing, refuse to put ourselves into a position to repeat adversity.

We should ask, "Why this?" until we get the best possible answer. Even as we do so, we must recognize that some problems and difficulties have no answer now. They may have an answer someday, especially as our understanding of God's universe increases. But the cause or cure for a particular disease may elude us today. We may never understand fully the motivation for another person to act the way she does. We may not have the capacity to comprehend all the factors that have contributed to a problem. We are not omniscient, and we never will be.

The best recourse is this: trust God for an answer that will bring you to a place of peace in your heart and mind. That is what you should pursue above all in asking the *why* questions related to adversity. Ask the Lord to give you an explanation to the best of your ability to receive and understand it, and then ask Him to give you the faith to trust His love and to rely on His all-knowing ability to undergird your life so that you have peace to cover your lack of understanding.

- *How do you feel about the fact that the Lord doesn't guarantee us adversity-free lives and He doesn't always give us a full or complete explanation for why certain things happen to us?*

_____

_____

If you continue to ask, "Why me?" you can tie yourself up in knots on the inside. You may begin to feel that God is picking on you, or that you are unworthy of God's love. You may get into a poor-me, pity-party syndrome or allow your self-esteem to be brought so low that you no longer have the motivation to reach out to others or minister to them. Don't let "why me?" questions dominate your thought life. If you do, you'll never really be able to get through the adversity that comes your way, much less advance in your spiritual relationship with the Lord through adversity.

- *Can you recall an experience in your life when you asked, "Why me?" Did you ever get a satisfactory answer? What would your answer be to the question "Why this?" regarding the same experience?*

_____

_____

Finding Someone on Whom to Lay Blame

The second question we tend to ask when adversity strikes is, "Who is responsible for this?" Our automatic tendency is to seek someone on whom to lay the blame for our trouble.

There are times when other people are at fault, at least to a degree, for the troubles we experience. But not all adversity is caused by, or is even related to, specific individuals we can name. Furthermore, most troubles are multifaceted; they nearly always involve more than one other person or one lone cause.

It's convenient, of course, for us to choose targets to blame for our adversity. Pointing a finger at another person is a form of denial about any involvement we might have had in creating the problem.

When we experience adversity, we must recognize that often, adversity comes as a result of our own doing. That's a hard fact to face, but we must do so if we are ever to mature in the Christian life.

Jesus' disciples were not completely off base in their concern about sin being the cause of a man's blindness (John 9:2–3). Sin sometimes is at the root of adversity.

Read this closely:

> Sin sometimes causes a problem, but not all problems are directly caused by an individual person's sin.

- *Can you recall an experience in your life, or the life of someone you know, in which sin caused adversity?*

———————————————————————————

———————————————————————————

- *Can you recall an experience in your life, or the life of someone you know, in which no sin seemed to be involved?*

———————————————————————————

———————————————————————————

We cannot assume, for example, that every person who has cancer has it as a result of sin. Conversely, we cannot say to a thief, "The fact that you stole that item and got caught for it is not your fault." Some willful actions on our part bring on calamity. Sin always results in adversity of some kind.

The book of James tells us, "But each one is tempted when he is drawn away by his own desires and enticed. Then, when desire has conceived, it gives birth to sin; and sin, when it is full-grown, brings forth death" (James 1:14–15). Sin always results in some form of death. Sometimes it is physical death, but usually, it is a much more subtle form of dying. Sin can cause relationships to die, self-esteem to die, and businesses to die. Certain sins kill ambition and discipline. All of these forms of death result in adversity to some degree.

Can you sin and not have that sin result in an adversity? No. The old phrase "be sure your sin will find you out" is true. Sin eventually erupts into visible and experiential adversity—sometimes sooner, sometimes later, but always inevitably.

The classic biblical example of the sure consequences of sin is the story of Adam and Eve. Their lives were free of adversity at the outset of their creation. Adam and Eve experienced no sickness, death, or suffering of any kind in the Garden of Eden. There was no tension in their relationship with each other. There was no conflict between them and their environment. They lived in a paradise and in complete harmony with God, each other, and nature.

Then things changed for one reason and only one reason—they sinned. They disobeyed God by eating of the fruit that God had explicitly forbidden them to eat. They knew what God had said. They knew they were disobeying. And they willfully chose to disobey. The consequence was far beyond our comprehension. From the moment they sinned, life for Adam and Eve became full of adversity; Eve experienced pain in bearing her children, man and woman had the potential for conflict in their relationship, and Adam struggled against his environment. And to top it all off, both faced living the rest of their days under the shadow of death.

It is into the fallen world caused by sin that each of us is born. The Scriptures teach us that sickness, pain, disease, famine, earthquakes, war, and death are part of the fallen state of the world. Thus, they are linked to the sin of Adam and Eve, and to the general sinfulness of the human race as a whole.

But what about specific examples of sin? Ultimately they are related in some way to the general sinful condition of the entire human race, and the general sinful condition of each human heart.

Follow this one example. A baby is sold into slavery. Why? Because the parents need money. Why? Because they and their older children are hungry. Why? Because there has been a severe famine in the land. Why? Because there has been no rain and the crops have died and there are no food reserves upon which to draw. Why? Because the farmers don't have good enough horticultural skills to produce abundant crops in order to have excess to store for times of emergency. Why? Because they haven't been taught farming skills. Why? Because those who have farming skills haven't shared them, and their leaders refuse to encourage the learning of these skills as a priority. Why? Because people are too busy pursuing other interests and desires. Why? Because people are motivated by greed, the lust of the eyes, the lust of the flesh, and the pride of life—all of which are self-centered and are aimed only at personal benefit (1 John 2:16). Why? Because people are sinful.

How many times in that one train of events does sin rear its ugly head? Certainly the parents sin when they sell their baby. But the sin of many others also is involved. Sin never affects only the person who commits it. It is like a stone thrown into a pond. It has a ripple effect. That's one of the main reasons we can err if we look at a person who is experiencing adversity and conclude unilaterally, "You and you alone have brought this onto your head."

The other side of the coin is this: sometimes we are the primary reason for our adversity. We err. We sin purposefully to gain our own way or to get what we want. We fail. We goof. We may act willfully or innocently, but sometimes we are at the core of our problem. We err when we conclude in our pride, "I had nothing to do with this problem!" The fact is, we likely contributed to the problem in some way, and we might have been the primary cause of the problem for reasons we haven't yet faced.

Until the time when you receive God's free gift of forgiveness into your personal life, you contribute to the "sin state" of the world, and you set up chains of events in your life that may bring about negative consequences long after you have accepted Jesus Christ as Savior. The decisions you make and the actions you take apart from the Lord set up situations in your life that aptly can be labeled as being adversity prone. Even after you acknowledge Jesus as Lord of your life, you are in the process of being transformed from a person who has operated according to sinful, human tendencies into a person who chooses godly righteousness at every turn. You never grow beyond your ability to be tempted or your ability to commit sin.

Galatians 6:7–8 states very clearly,

> Do not be deceived, God is not mocked; for whatever a man sows, that he will also reap. For he who sows to his flesh will of the flesh reap corruption, but he who sows to the Spirit will of the Spirit reap everlasting life.

In sum, you help create adversity by your sinful behavior—directly or indirectly, with immediate or long-range results. You must face that fact squarely.

If you deny your role in a problem for which you are partly, primarily, or even solely responsible, you are living in a state of denial, which is a state of untruth.

John 8:31–32 cites these words of Jesus: "If you abide in My word, you are My disciples indeed. And you shall know the truth, and the truth shall make you free." Only the truth can set you free and bring about complete healing, lasting restitution, and a sure solution. Not only that, but truth is a necessity if you are to avoid re-creating the problem in the future.

Don't deny your part in adversity. Face up to it. And ask the Lord to forgive you for your error, sin, or mistake. That's the only way you can begin to advance through this problem and grow into greater perfection in the Lord.

- *Recall a time of adversity in your life. Did you attempt to assign blame to someone? Did you ever reach the place of accepting your role or responsibility for the situation? Why is it easier to blame someone else for a problem? Why is it wrong to do so?*

_____

_____

- *Can you recall a time in which you know, in your heart of hearts, that you were the cause of adversity?*

_____

_____

- *Can you recall a time in your life, or the life of someone else, in which decisions or actions taken prior to a person's acceptance of Jesus Christ as Savior and Lord resulted in adverse consequences even after becoming a Christian?*

_____

_____

What About Blaming Adversity on Satan?

A number of years ago the expression "the devil made me do it" was quite popular. That wasn't a new idea, of course. Eve tried that excuse in the Garden of Eden!

Blaming the devil for every bit of adversity that we experience is a convenient means of self-justification. Many people make the devil their scapegoat. They refuse to be responsible for anything bad that comes their way. But again, that's living in denial. The devil probably doesn't deserve as much credit as we give him.

Am I denying the power of Satan? No. Satan is real, alive, and active in our world today. He is 100 percent evil, and everything he does is intended to steal from, kill, or destroy God's children (John 10:10). I *am* saying that we err if we blame Satan for every problem or need in our lives to the point that we deny our sin or deny that something or someone other than Satan may have been a factor in our adversity.

Satan may be the father of all lies and the instigator of all temptation, but he is not the father of all adversity. We human beings do a pretty good job of bringing about adversity on our own, even without direct help from Satan.

There are times when people open themselves up to evil so that they experience intense oppression, or even possession, by demons. The times are rare, however, and the influence of demons generally intensifies as willful, sinful behavior progresses over time. In the vast majority of cases, the devil does not make us do it when it comes to sinful behavior. The devil tempts, and we do the sinning!

At other times Satan is a direct source of adversity. He is clearly called our "adversary" in the Scriptures, a name directly linked to adversity. The clearest example in the Bible is the story of Job.

Job's friends and family came to him repeatedly, trying to link Job's adversity to his sin or lack of faith. The Bible says, however, that Job was "blameless and upright, and one who feared God and shunned evil" (Job 1:1). From God's perspective, Job was a model of human righteousness (Job 1:8).

Satan, however, argued with God that Job was righteous only because God had blessed him in many wonderful ways. So the Lord said, "Behold, all that he has is in your power; only do not lay a hand on his person" (Job 1:12). So Satan set out to destroy all Job had, and Job continued to serve God and walk in His ways.

Satan then made another request: "Skin for skin! Yes, all that a man has he will give for his life. But stretch out Your hand now, and touch his bone and his flesh, and he will surely curse You to Your face!" And the Lord said to Satan, "Behold, he is in your hand, but spare his life" (Job 2:4–6).

Satan then struck Job with painful boils. Note that although God gave permission for Satan to strike Job, the striking itself and the motivation for the adversity came from Satan.

Satan is the ultimate enemy of our souls. Spiritual torment comes from him. In many ways, this form of adversity is the most painful and personal—those who experience this form of torment usually are filled with fear, plagued with doubts, and never at peace. The solution for this type of adversity is the same as the solution for all types of adversity in which Satan has a direct hand: turn to God and trust Him with our lives.

Which brings us back to our second main question that we ask in times of adversity, "Who is responsible for this adversity?"

The answer is, sometimes we are, sometimes others are, sometimes the devil is, sometimes it's a mix (ourselves, others, Satan), and sometimes, as we will discuss in a future lesson, the instigator of the adversity may be God Himself.

When we ask, "Who is responsible?" we may derive some benefit in identifying the root source or sources of the adversity. We certainly may benefit from knowing whom to avoid, what to change in our lives and relationships, or how to withstand Satan more effectively. In the end, we must come to the conclusion that regardless of who is responsible for our being in a state of adversity, only one Person truly can help us out of our adversity: the Lord Jesus Christ. He is our sure help in times of trouble. As Psalm 46:1 declares, "God is our refuge and strength, a very present help in trouble."

We also must recognize that just as in the case of the "why me?" question, the answer to the "who is responsible?" question may elude us to some degree. We may never know fully who is responsible, from God's perspective, for the trouble in which we find ourselves. But we can know the source of our solution, our answer, our healing, our deliverance, our redemption, our salvation. His name is Jesus.

This brings us then to the question that we *should* ask in times of adversity . . .

How Should I Respond to This Adversity?

"Why did this happen?" and "Who is responsible?" cause us to look from our adversity backward into our lives and past events. Asking, "How should I respond to this adversity?" turns our focus forward. It is the most productive, helpful, and positive response we can make in a time of trouble.

The disciples of Jesus no doubt stood at Calvary wondering why such a horrible thing as the crucifixion of their Master had taken place. Humanly speaking, the crucifixion of Jesus made no sense at all to them. Their dreams were shattered. They had seen their beloved leader suffer and die before their very eyes.

The disciples might well have asked, "Who was responsible for this?" Roman or Jewish leaders? The clamoring crowd that had been so easily assembled and whipped into a frenzy? Sin? Satan? God? The answer is yes to all!

Yet Christ's response to the heavenly Father was to allow God to use a terrible form of adversity to fulfill God's plan of salvation and to achieve an eternal and marvelous good.

And that's the response you are to have today. When adversity strikes, you are to boldly face the situation and your future and ask, "What now?" You must avoid the tendency to get bogged down in an endless pursuit of an answer to the "who is responsible for this trouble?" question and turn your focus on the answer to a much more positive, forward-looking question, "Who can bring me out of this trouble and turn things to good in my life?"

The only way you can advance in your spiritual life in times of adversity is to look up to Jesus and forward into your future with Him. He ultimately is the answer to the *why* and *who* questions you ask!

- *What new insights do you have into the nature of adversity as the result of this lesson?*

_____

_____

IS ADVERSITY EVER CAUSED BY GOD?

Does God ever cause adversity in our lives?

The comfortable, but theologically incorrect, answer is no. You will find many people preaching and teaching that God never sends an ill wind into a person's life, but that position can't be justified by Scripture. The Bible teaches that God does send adversity—but within certain parameters and always for a reason that relates to our growth, perfection, and eternal good.

Does this make God any less a loving, good God? No. Neither is a parent who disciplines a child any less a loving, good parent. In fact, the consistent and positive discipline of a child is a hallmark of good parenting. In like fashion, the disciplining actions of God are part of His attribute of flawless goodness. A good and loving God would do nothing less than discipline His children for their benefit.

Consider the life of Paul the apostle. There can be no doubt that the Lord greatly loved him. God called him in a dramatic and direct way to become an apostle to the gentile world. Paul knew the Lord intimately, and he followed Him explicitly. But that does not mean that Paul was spared all adversity.

Some of the adversity that Paul faced was no doubt of his own doing. He was a bold man who refused to compromise and who likely ruffled some feathers along the way.

Much of the adversity was caused by others—those who refused his ministry and who persecuted him with beatings, floggings, imprisonment, and stonings, even to the point of attempting to kill him. Paul also said he was robbed on occasion. False brethren and his own countrymen attempted to harm him.

Some of the adversity was encountered as he traveled and ministered in foreign places—storms, weariness and toil, sleeplessness, cold, hunger and thirst.

Some of the adversity was no doubt caused by Satan, who attempted to destroy Paul at every turn.

In 2 Corinthians 11:23–28, Paul listed the adversities he faced in the course of his ministry. Given even a fraction of that list, most people would probably have given up and said, "Let somebody else take a turn at being an apostle." But not Paul. His great love and concern for the Lord and the churches he had established drove him forward.

"But," you may say, "I see no mention of adversity caused by God in the list of Paul's struggles."

Read on.

In 2 Corinthians 12:7–10, Paul wrote,

> And lest I should be exalted above measure by the abundance of the revelations, a thorn in the flesh was given to me, a messenger of Satan to buffet me, lest I be exalted above measure. Concerning this thing I pleaded with the Lord three times that it might depart from me. And He said to me, "My grace is sufficient for you, for My strength is made perfect in weakness." Therefore most gladly I will rather boast in my infirmities, that the power of Christ may rest upon me. Therefore I take pleasure in infirmities, in reproaches, in needs, in persecution, in distresses, for Christ's sake. For when I am weak, then I am strong.

Many people have speculated about the exact nature of Paul's "thorn in the flesh," but we don't know what it was. God doesn't tell us in His Word. I think there is probably a very good reason for that. If we knew the nature of Paul's thorn in the flesh, then any person who experienced that same ailment or form of attack would say, "Well, I have the same thing Paul had." That could be a cause for boasting by some or a false explanation for a problem by others.

We do know these things about Paul's thorn in the flesh:

- *It was given to him.* Paul concluded that a "messenger from Satan" delivered the gift, but that the giver of the adversity was the Lord Himself.
- *It was for a purpose.* Paul pleaded with the Lord to take back the gift, but the Lord refused, saying, in essence, "I have a purpose for this in your life."
- *It was for Paul's ultimate good.* Even as Paul began describing the gift of God, he noted that it was for a specific purpose: "Lest I should be exalted above measure by the abundance of the revelations." Paul was referring to visions and revelations he received from the Lord, including one in which he was caught up to heaven (2 Cor. 12:1–4). Paul perceived that the Lord had given him a thorn in the flesh so that he wouldn't be "exalted above measure" and so that the Lord might be seen as the sole cause for anything that might be called successful ministry in Paul's life.

We know Paul regarded the thorn in the flesh as coming from the Lord because he did not deal with it in the same way that he dealt with satanic attack, persecution, or his own sinfulness. When confronted by demons or satanic attack, Paul rebuked the enemy soundly and brought deliverance to those who were under Satan's influence. Paul stood up to persecutors, and he had no fear when it came to confronting them or arguing with them. Throughout his letters in the New Testament, Paul was quick to acknowledge his own past sinful nature. But in this instance Paul reported a conversation with the Lord. Paul acknowledged that the Lord had a purpose in giving a thorn in the flesh to him and that he was submissive to the purpose.

Being submissive to God's chastisement or adversity isn't easy. The first response to adversity is to attempt to flee from it or shake it off. It takes a certain amount of spiritual maturity to admit, "God may have a message for me in this adversity. He may be trying to deal with me in some way so that I might grow in my faith and become more like Jesus."

There are four great truths that I want you to consider in this lesson:

1. You can never see the beginning from the ending of God's plan for your life, but God sees the big picture and all the details that are a part of it.
2. All adversity in your life must be sifted first through the permissive will of God.
3. God will not test you beyond your ability to endure.
4. God's full help in times of adversity is available only to the Christian.

God's Plan for Your Life

God has a plan and a purpose for your life as a whole. He is continually in the process of preparing you to be a person with whom He intends to live forever. In day-to-day life, God has a plan and a purpose for everything that becomes a part of your life or that affects your life.

God's love for you is far greater than anything you can ask or imagine. He has at His disposal an infinite number of ways of bringing you to new levels of maturity in Christ Jesus. He knows who, and what, to bring into your life at any given moment in order to accomplish His very specific goals in your life.

Sometimes the only way some of us will submit ourselves to God's plan is for us to experience anguish, pressure, trials, tribulations, or heartaches. If that is the case, the Lord will use adversity to lead us to a place in the spiritual life where we will turn to Him, trust Him more, be healed in areas where we need healing, and grow in ways we need to grow.

There is an old saying,

> *God whispers in our pleasure.*
> *God speaks in our conscience.*
> *God shouts in our pain.*
> *And He really gets our attention when*
> *the pain is intense and beyond our control.*

I have seen the reality of that saying in my life and in the lives of countless people I know.

You cannot know God's full plan for your life. From time to time, you may have glimpses of what God still has in store for you to become or do. You are finite. God is infinite. He alone can see the full scope of your life and how you fit into His plan for the ages.

Because God is infinite, omnipotent (all-powerful), omniscient (all-knowing), omnipresent (ever-present and eternal), and totally loving, we can trust Him to know how each experience, circumstance, and relationship in our lives fits into God's plan. We may not see any purpose for some of the troubles that come our way. But God always sees purpose in everything, and furthermore, He sees an eternal purpose.

Your first response when adversity comes must be to trust God to make a way through the adversity, to trust God to have a "perfecting good" for you as a result of the adversity, and to trust God that there is an eternal purpose for the adversity.

What the Word Says	What the Word Says to Me
"For My thoughts are not your thoughts,	_____
Nor are your ways My ways,"	_____
says the LORD.	_____
"For as the heavens are higher	_____
than the earth,	_____

So are My ways higher than your
ways,
And My thoughts than your
thoughts" (Isa. 55:8–9).

Trust in the LORD with all your
heart,
And lean not on your own under-
standing;
In all your ways acknowledge
Him,
And He shall direct your paths
(Prov. 3:5–6).

God Gives the Permission

In an earlier lesson I referred briefly to Job and to how the Lord gave permission to Satan on two occasions to test Job—once regarding his possessions and children, and a second time regarding Job's personal health and well-being.

The life story of Joseph, son of Jacob, is another lesson for us in understanding God's granting permission for adversity to enter our lives so that an ultimate good might be accomplished.

Joseph was greatly loved by his father, a fact that caused his brothers to be jealous. When Joseph shared two dreams with his brothers—in which Joseph was exalted and his brothers bowed to serve him—that was more than the brothers could take. Even though Jacob rebuked Joseph for telling the dreams, the brothers were determined to teach Joseph a lesson (Gen. 37:1–10).

Joseph got lost on his way to find his brothers, but he encountered a man in the wilderness who directed him to them at Dothan. When he finally arrived at the place where his brothers were tending their flocks, the brothers conspired first to kill him, and then to strip him of his tunic and throw him into an empty, waterless pit. When a caravan of Midianite traders came along, they sold Joseph to them. The Midianites, in turn, sold Joseph as a slave to Potiphar, an officer of Pharaoh (Gen. 37:11–28, 36).

Joseph rose to prominence in Potiphar's house, but the advances and false accusations of Potiphar's wife landed him in prison. Joseph rose in leadership among the prisoners, but the chief butler he aided in prison forgot him for two full years before he mentioned him to Pharaoh (Gen. 39—40).

Talk about a long string of adverse situations! Few of us have ever been so persecuted by our family members, and then an employer, and then a peer. Joseph endured adversity year after year after year.

Then, in a day, Joseph's destiny was fulfilled. His adversity was reversed. Joseph interpreted a dream for Pharaoh and was put in charge of the nation's harvest, an important and prominent position. He was given Pharaoh's signet ring in order to conduct business in Pharaoh's name. He was given a chariot and a gold chain that indicated to the entire nation that Joseph was second in command to Pharaoh—in other words, the prime minister of the land. What a day that must have been in Joseph's life! It surely must have felt like a dream to him.

Later, Joseph was able to help his family in a time of severe famine. In the course of Joseph's saving their lives, his brothers did bow down to Joseph (Gen. 41—47, 50).

After Jacob's death, the brothers feared for their lives for what they had done to Joseph in selling him to the Midianites, but Joseph said to them, "Do not be afraid, for am I in the place of God? But as for you, you meant evil against me; but God meant it for good, in order to bring it about as it is this day, to save many people alive" (Gen. 50:19–20).

Joseph concluded in looking back over the events of his life that God had been in charge all the time. Nothing had happened to him that was apart from God's permissive will. All the events of his life were part of a divine plan. Some Bible scholars conclude that the "man" who directed Joseph to his brothers at Dothan was an angel of the Lord—if so, the man was directing Joseph to the very brothers who would sell him into slavery.

Did God desire for Joseph to be subjected to such adversity? The Scriptures don't say that directly. But we can conclude that God permitted the adverse situations in Joseph's life. The Scriptures tell us that Joseph trusted the Lord continually. The adversity had nothing to do with judgment on Joseph, nor was it a form of chastisement.

Certainly, the Lord could have put a stop to the adversity at numerous points. The Lord could have stopped Jacob from sending Joseph to his brothers. He could have stopped a man from telling Joseph where to find his brothers. He could have averted the travel plans of the Midianites, or allowed Joseph to escape from their hands. He could have provided witnesses to counteract the false claims of Potiphar's wife. He could have caused the chief butler to remember Joseph sooner. And these are only a few of the ways in which the Lord could have stopped adversity from coming into Joseph's life or intervened to stop it. Instead, the Lord chose to allow Joseph to endure the hardships.

Finally, the Scriptures tell us that the Lord was *with* Joseph in each and every experience, and that He blessed Joseph *in spite of* adverse circumstances. That's good news for us as we face adversity! When we look at Joseph's life as a whole, we see that he moved from strength to even greater strength. Each adverse situation prepared him in some way for the leadership role he was going to assume eventually. Joseph didn't bow down to defeat; rather, those who sought to defeat Joseph bowed down to him. We can trust for the same outcome.

When you belong to the Lord, any adversity that you experience is subject to the Lord's power and grace. He never stops being in charge of your life. He never loses authority over you or over the circumstances that affect you. God is always in control.

Therefore, you must draw the conclusion that the Lord allows, or permits, adversity to enter your life on occasion. He uses adversity to fulfill His purposes in you and through you. Joseph's destiny wasn't limited to Joseph, or even to Joseph and his family. It involved all the tribes of Israel and the destiny of a nation.

What the Word Says	What the Word Says to Me
God sent me before you to preserve a posterity for you in the	_____ _____

earth, and to save your lives by a
great deliverance. So now it was
not you who sent me here, but
God (Gen. 45:7–8).

_____
_____
_____
_____

Do not lead us into temptation,
but deliver us from the evil one
(Matt. 6:13).

_____
_____
_____

O LORD, do not rebuke me in
Your wrath,
Nor chasten me in Your hot dis-
pleasure!
For Your arrows pierce me
deeply,
And Your hand presses me down
(Ps. 38:1–2).

_____
_____
_____
_____
_____
_____
_____

God Limits Adversity

Although God may allow Satan to persecute us and harass us, God also puts a limit on the amount of adversity He allows Satan to send our way. In the case of Job, the Lord stopped Satan the first time with the limitation of "do not lay a hand on his person" (Job 1:12), and the second time with the limitation of "spare his life" (Job 2:6). Satan had to comply with God's command both times, and Satan has to comply today with God's limitations on the amount of adversity you and I experience as God's children.

That's good news for us. There is a limit to adversity. It will come to an end.

A woman said to me that one of her favorite phrases in the Bible was "and it came to pass." She said, "Just think, it came to pass. It didn't come to stay!" That's a good attitude to have about adversity.

Today's troubles are just that—*today's* troubles. A season of trouble is just that—a season of trouble. Crises pass. Circumstances change. Situations evolve. God works in and through adversity to bring it to an end according to His timetable.

Daniel noted this in his prophetic word when he said that the "beast" would be allowed to persecute the saints "for a time and times and half a time" (Dan. 7:23–25). The word *persecute* in this passage literally means "wear out." The enemy of our souls attempts to grind us down, wear us out, wring us dry. But God says, "Not completely." There is nothing Satan can do to us or in us beyond a point if we will continue to trust God and resist the devil.

Furthermore, the Lord does not allow us to be tempted or persecuted beyond our ability to endure it:

> No temptation has overtaken you except such as is common to man; but God is faithful, who will not allow you to be tempted beyond what you are able, but with the temptation will also make the way of escape, that you may be able to bear it (1 Cor. 10:13).

What good news this is! God will provide a way of escape from our trials and tribulations.

What the Word Says	What the Word Says to Me
He who endures to the end will be saved (Matt. 10:22).	_____ _____
The fourth beast . . . shall speak pompous words against the Most High,	_____ _____ _____
Shall persecute the saints of the Most High,	_____ _____
And shall intend to change times and law.	_____ _____
Then the saints shall be given into his hand	_____ _____
For a time and times and half a time (Dan. 7:23–25).	_____ _____

"Go up on her walls and destroy,
But do not make a complete end.
Take away her branches,
For they are not the LORD's.
For the house of Israel and the
house of Judah
Have dealt very treacherously
with Me," says the LORD (Jer.
5:10–11).

_____
_____
_____
_____
_____
_____
_____
_____

God's Help Is to the Believer

The Lord uses adversity in the life of the believer for many purposes, all of them ultimately good. He limits adversity in the life of the believer and provides a way of escape. But none of these statements can be made on behalf of the unbeliever.

The unbeliever stands before God in an enemy position—a position of estrangement and alienation. The unbeliever is loved, but also is subject to harsh treatment if she confronts God's children or attempts to interfere with God's plans.

Time and again in the Scriptures we read where God showed no mercy to His enemies. He defeated them soundly and decisively, and He commanded the Israelites on a number of occasions "to destroy utterly" their enemies. To be an enemy of God is to be in a very precarious position. Not only is the unsaved person in a spiritually lost state, but he is in danger physically, emotionally, and mentally. The enemy has total access to an unbeliever, limited only by the prayers of God's faithful people on behalf of that person.

God's response to the unsaved person is a response to the person's willful sin and acts of transgression. The Lord does not sit on His throne and survey the world and take potshots at people in a willy-nilly, capricious manner. He sets out to show that He is in control. God is not a bully. Rather, the Lord moves against sin. God is just and righteous. He _must_ counteract sin.

That is the message of Jeremiah in the book of Lamentations

when he concludes that the Lord does not "afflict willingly." The Lord does not will adversity for His people; rather, He is responsive to our actions. And when we sin, God responds to our sin even as He loves us beyond measure.

What the Word Says	What the Word Says to Me
And the fear of God was on all the kingdoms of those countries when they heard that the LORD had fought against the enemies of Israel (2 Chron. 20:29).	_____ _____ _____ _____ _____
"And I will come near you for judgment; I will be a swift witness Against sorcerers, Against adulterers, Against perjurers, Against those who exploit wage earners and widows and orphans, And against those who turn away an alien— Because they do not fear Me," Says the LORD of hosts (Mal. 3:5).	_____ _____ _____ _____ _____ _____ _____ _____ _____ _____ _____
The LORD tests the righteous, But the wicked and the one who loves violence His soul hates (Ps. 11:5).	_____ _____ _____ _____
For the Lord will not cast off forever. Though He causes grief, Yet He will show compassion	_____ _____ _____ _____

According to the multitude of

His mercies.

For He does not afflict willingly,

Nor grieve the children of men

(Lam. 3:31–33).

_____

_____

_____

_____

_____

Your Response When God Sends Adversity

Your quick response should be threefold when adversity is God's choice of tool to build His character into you.

"Deliver me!" That is repeatedly the cry of God's people throughout the Scriptures. Pray for God's speedy deliverance from adversity.

"Thank You, Lord." You must acknowledge to the Lord that you realize that He may be dealing with you to show you something in your life that needs to be changed, or something that you need to do so that you might become more like His Son, Jesus Christ.

"I trust You, Lord." As you yield to what the Lord desires to accomplish in your life, you must rest in faith that God has a plan and that He is in control—and that His hand on your life is one of unconditional love and omnipotent power over the adversity or messenger of adversity.

- *What new insights do you have about the nature of adversity and how to respond to it?*

  _____

  _____

- *Can you recall a time in your life when, in looking back on the situation, you see how the Lord might have permitted adversity to bring about a great good in your life or the life of someone you know?*

  _____

  _____

LESSON 4

THREE REASONS GOD ALLOWS ADVERSITY

If we are willing to acknowledge that adversity can bring about something positive in our lives, and that God desires for adversity to have a good and beneficial purpose in making us more like Jesus Christ, then we must ask ourselves a question when a crisis hits: What reasons may the Lord have for this adversity in my life?

Adversity, anguish, trials, tribulations, and heartaches operate as lessons in the school of experience. They bring us to a place of new insight and understanding; they can alter our perception of the world and of God, and lead us to change our behavior. The Lord, of course, is the ultimate Teacher. He is the One to whom we must look for the meaning of any lesson related to adversity.

God allows adversity for three reasons:

1. To get our attention.
2. To lead us into self-examination.
3. To bring us to a place where we will change our belief or our behavior.

1. God Uses Adversity to Get Our Attention

As any teacher in a classroom or Sunday school can tell you, the first goal of a teacher is to get a student's attention. You can't teach a student who isn't listening or paying attention. The Lord sometimes uses adversity in our lives to cause us to pay attention to Him in a new way.

That is what happened to Saul of Tarsus as he traveled on the road to Damascus. He intended to bring great persecution upon the Christians in that city. It was not a routine bureaucratic trip for Saul. The Scriptures tell us that Saul was "breathing threats and murder against the disciples of the Lord" (Acts 9:1). Saul was so much given to his task that he was nearly consumed by his murderous intent.

However, God got Saul's attention as he made his way to Damascus:

> As he journeyed he came near Damascus, and suddenly a light shone around him from heaven. Then he fell to the ground, and heard a voice saying to him, "Saul, Saul, why are you persecuting Me?" And he said, "Who are You, Lord?" Then the Lord said, "I am Jesus, whom you are persecuting. It is hard for you to kick against the goads." So he, trembling and astonished, said, "Lord, what do You want me to do?" Then the Lord said to him, "Arise and go into the city, and you will be told what you must do." . . . Then Saul arose from the ground, and when his eyes were opened he saw no one. But they led him by the hand and brought him into Damascus (Acts 9:3–6, 8).

Saul definitely had a wake-up call from the Lord that day. In one unforeseen moment, God gained Saul's undivided attention, striking him with the adversity of blindness and no doubt humiliating him in front of his traveling companions as he groveled in the dust of the road. But God had Saul exactly where He wanted him. Saul was more than ready to listen when the Lord asked, "Why are you persecuting Me?" Up to that point, Saul perhaps had thought he was only persecuting Christians, not the Lord

Himself. A period of intense adversity resulted in a complete turnaround for Saul, to the point that he was proclaiming Jesus in the synagogues within a matter of days (Acts 9:20).

When we read or hear a story such as this one, it is easy to see the value of adversity. If it took temporary blindness and humiliation to get Saul's attention, it was certainly worth it, for through Saul—known to us as Paul the apostle—the gospel was preached and churches were planted across the Roman world.

One of the best responses I know to adversity that strikes us suddenly and yet obviously with a God-intended message is to turn to Psalm 25 and make it our personal prayer:

> *To You, O LORD, I lift up my soul.*
> *O my God, I trust in You;*
> *Let me not be ashamed;*
> *Let not my enemies triumph over me.*
> *Indeed, let no one who waits on You be ashamed;*
> *Let those be ashamed who deal treacherously without cause.*
> *Show me Your ways, O LORD;*
> *Teach me Your paths.*
> *Lead me in Your truth and teach me,*
> *For You are the God of my salvation;*
> *On You I wait all the day.*
> *Remember, O LORD, Your tender mercies and Your*
> *   lovingkindnesses,*
> *For they are from of old.*
> *Do not remember the sins of my youth, nor my transgressions;*
> *According to Your mercy remember me,*
> *For Your goodness' sake, O LORD (vv. 1–7).*

Don't delay in responding to the Lord when He makes a move to get your attention. Respond quickly and humbly. Hear what He has to say to you.

What the Word Says	What the Word Says to Me
Then the LORD opened Balaam's eyes, and he saw the Angel of the	_____ _____

LORD standing in the way with His drawn sword in His hand; and he bowed his head and fell flat on his face. And the Angel of the LORD said to him, "Why have you struck your donkey these three times? Behold, I have come out to stand against you, because your way is perverse before Me. The donkey saw Me and turned aside from Me these three times. If she had not turned aside from Me, surely I would also have killed you by now, and let her live." And Balaam said to the Angel of the LORD, "I have sinned, for I did not know You stood in the way against me. Now therefore, if it displeases You, I will turn back" (Num. 22:31–34).

Eli said to Samuel, "Go, lie down; and it shall be, if He calls you, that you must say, 'Speak, LORD, for Your servant hears.'" So Samuel went and lay down in his place. Now the LORD came and stood and called as at other times, "Samuel! Samuel!" And Samuel answered, "Speak, for Your servant hears" (1 Sam. 3:9–10).

2. Adversity Leads to Examination

At times God sees fit to allow a little adversity into our lives to motivate us to self-examination. The winds of adversity blow off the surface issues and force us to cope with things on a deeper level. Adversity removes the cloak of what we are supposed to be to reveal the truth of who we are. The "real us" shows through.

As Christians, we are to be about this activity of self-examination in an ongoing, regular way. Paul encouraged the Corinthians, "Let a man examine himself" (1 Cor. 11:28). In other words, "Take an inquisitive look inside and discover what is driving you, motivating you, and enticing you."

God does not want negative elements from the past to lie around in our lives and cause us to deteriorate. Each of us is the temple of the Holy Spirit, and He wants us to be clean and usable vessels. There is no reason to allow the rubbish of the past to remain in our lives for years—old memories, haunting temptations, the baggage of unresolved hurts and unreconciled relationships. The Lord desires that we be free of anything that might keep us in inner bondage—mentally, emotionally, psychologically, or spiritually. When we become complacent in accepting the hurts of the past as part of who we are, the Lord may bring a little adversity to lead us to face who we are and pursue instead who we *might* be in Christ Jesus.

The longer we allow important spiritual issues to go unresolved, the greater their negative potential. The deeper the roots, the greater our resistance and the more painful the excavation process. That is one of the reasons God keeps the pressure on us. He knows that if He lets up, we will return to our old ways.

What the Word Says	What the Word Says to Me
Search me, O God, and know my heart;	_____
Try me, and know my anxieties;	_____
And see if there is any wicked	_____

way in me,
And lead me in the way everlasting (Ps. 139:23–24).

_____

_____

_____

Let us search out and examine
our ways,
And turn back to the LORD;
Let us lift our hearts and hands
To God in heaven (Lam. 3:40–
41).

_____

_____

_____

_____

_____

_____

The spirit of a man is the lamp of
the LORD,
Searching all the inner depths of
his heart (Prov. 20:27).

_____

_____

_____

_____

3. The Effective Lesson Leads to Change in Behavior

Teachers often prepare behavioral objectives for their classroom lessons. These objectives list in concrete and measurable form the behaviors that the teacher desires for a student to manifest as proof that the student has learned the lesson. The lessons that the Lord teaches us through adversity are ultimately for that same purpose: a change in behavior, including a change in the belief that gives rise to behavior.

It isn't enough that the Lord gets our attention or that we engage in self-examination. We can see a problem and know ourselves thoroughly, but unless we change our response to God in some way, we will never benefit fully from adversity or grow as a result of it.

Self-examination may be a painful experience for you. But remember, whatever you find within yourself, Jesus Himself came to help you carry that burden to the cross and deal with it there once and for all. He has your best interest in mind. He knows that pain sometimes paves the path to complete healing and restoration of the inner person.

If you are willing to allow God to surface the inner rubbish of your life, and if you are willing to change what needs to be changed in your life, you will emerge from adversity closer to Christ, more mature as His child, and with far greater potential to reflect the love of God to the world around you.

What the Word Says	What the Word Says to Me
Hear, my children, the instruction of a father,	
And give attention to know understanding;	
For I give you good doctrine:	
Do not forsake my law. . . .	
"Let your heart retain my words;	
Keep my commands, and live"	
(Prov. 4:1–2, 4).	
Blessed is the man	
Who walks not in the counsel of the ungodly,	
Nor stands in the path of sinners,	
Nor sits in the seat of the scornful;	
But his delight is in the law of the LORD,	
And in His law he meditates day and night.	
He shall be like a tree	
Planted by the rivers of water,	
That brings forth its fruit in its season,	
Whose leaf also shall not wither;	

And whatever he does shall prosper (Ps. 1:1–3).

_____

_____

Let us cast off the works of dark-
ness, and let us put on the armor
of light. Let us walk properly, as
in the day, not in revelry and
drunkenness, not in lewdness
and lust, not in strife and envy.
But put on the Lord Jesus Christ,
and make no provision for the
flesh, to fulfill its lusts (Rom.
13:12–14).

_____

_____

_____

_____

_____

_____

_____

_____

_____

_____

Our Continual Growth Is the Lord's Desire

The Lord has made no provision for any of us to stop at some point in our growth toward full wholeness as human beings. We may never fully arrive at the perfection of Christ Jesus, but we are always to be growing more like Him. We must never become complacent about who we are or be satisfied that we have developed all the character that is necessary. Character building and spiritual maturity are both lifelong processes.

When we become complacent, the Lord may permit adversity to come our way in order to jostle us forward in our spiritual walk. God doesn't merely seek to get the attention of sinners; He also desires to have the full attention of those who love Him. God compels all of us to engage in periodic self-examination so we may face up to our own sin and the smudges on the soul that we acquire in the course of our lives. And always, the Lord desires that we do the difficult work of changing our beliefs and our behavior so that what we believe and do are in total harmony with what Jesus would believe and do if He were walking in our shoes today.

Move forward. Keep growing. Never stop looking forward and upward to Christ Jesus.

- *Can you recall an experience in your life in which you believe the Lord got your attention? How did you feel? How did you respond? What was the outcome?*

  _____

  _____

- *Can you recall an experience in which you believe the Lord led you to examine a particular area of your life in a specific and focused way? Was it a painful experience for you? How did you respond? What was the result?*

  _____

  _____

FOUR CORRECTIONS ADVERSITY COMPELS US TO MAKE

Have you ever been on a journey in which you needed to make a midcourse correction? Pilots make course corrections often as they maneuver through air traffic patterns and avoid potential storms. Road construction crews and detours sometimes force us to make course corrections when we travel by car.

The same principle holds true for life's journey. There are times when we need to make course corrections in order to arrive safely and soundly at our next spiritual destination point and ultimately to heaven. Adversity may be the detour, storm, or obstacle that compels us to make such corrections.

The Lord always requires His beloved children to make changes in at least four areas. The Lord is insistent that we (1) conquer pride and humble ourselves to the Lord's will, (2) come to the place where we hate sin and purge ourselves of evil, (3) sift our friendships so that they are in keeping with God's plan for our lives, and (4) adjust our priorities so that we place highest value on the things of God and, in turn, adopt new habits of behavior based on right priorities.

Sometimes pride, sin, harmful relationships, and wrong priorities are so deeply embedded within us that we can hardly recognize them in ourselves. That is a dangerous blindness. A primary reason to read our Bibles on a daily basis is to encounter repeatedly God's directives and desires for our lives. Anytime you read your Bible, you should pray, "Show me, Lord, how this affects my life," or "Reveal to me, Lord, how I need to change my life in order to conform to Your commandments and Your will."

As we enter into this lesson on God's use of adversity to bring about midcourse corrections in our lives, we also need to recognize anew that the Lord corrects us because He loves us. Proverbs 3:12 is an important verse to memorize: "Whom the LORD loves He corrects, just as a father the son in whom he delights."

A good parent guides a child's behavior—continually teaching the child what is good, acceptable, and beneficial, and what is bad, unacceptable, and harmful. If a parent doesn't do this for a child, a child grows up to be wild in behavior, and that wildness makes him miserable in himself, undesired by others, and alienated from those who might bless or help him the most. In like manner, God desires for us to be disciplined and mature adults in the faith so that we might experience inner peace and harmony, enjoy relationships with other believers, and receive the blessings that God desires to give to us through other people.

- *Can you recall an experience in your life in which your parents corrected your behavior for your good?*

Another reason the Lord corrects us is so that we may be fruitful. Jesus taught this point using the analogy of a vine and its branches:

I am the true vine, and My Father is the vinedresser. Every branch in Me that does not bear fruit He takes away; and every branch that bears fruit He prunes, that it may bear more fruit. . . . I am the vine, you are the branches. He who abides in Me, and I in him, bears much fruit; for without Me you can do nothing. If anyone does not abide in Me, he is cast out as a branch and is withered. . . . If you abide in Me, and My words abide in you, you will ask what you desire, and it shall be done for you. By this My Father is glorified, that you bear much fruit; so you will be My disciples (John 15:1–8).

God, our heavenly Father, is the vinedresser. He prunes us—and will continue to prune us—so that everything in our lives bears fruit or, in other words, is beneficial to His eternal purposes. Whatever He cuts away from our lives, even though it may involve the pain of adversity or trial, is for our benefit. It's dead wood as far as the Lord is concerned, and dead wood occupies space—or in the case of our lives, our time and energy—that could be occupied by fruit-bearing activities. Furthermore, the Lord says that in abiding in Him and His Word, and in bearing fruit, we are His disciples.

Just as the pruning of vines is important to their fruitfulness, so the Lord's correction is necessary for us to accomplish our God-given purpose in life and to find deep inner fulfillment.

Rather than shudder at the thought of the Lord's pruning, we should rejoice. We are about to be liberated of all dead weight and falsehood that may keep us from blessings.

1. Correcting Our Attitude of Pride

The Lord hates human pride. James 4:6 states very clearly, "God resists the proud, but gives grace to the humble." In fact, we have this same message three times in the Scriptures. (See also Prov. 3:34 and 1 Peter 5:5.)

Elsewhere, pride is listed among four things that the Lord hates: pride, arrogance, the evil way, and the perverse mouth

(Prov. 8:13). In yet another passage of Scripture, pride is listed among seven things that are an abomination to God:

> *A proud look,*
> *A lying tongue,*
> *Hands that shed innocent blood,*
> *A heart that devises wicked plans,*
> *Feet that are swift in running to evil,*
> *A false witness who speaks lies,*
> *And one who sows discord among brethren*
> *(Prov. 6:17–19).*

Pride is in the same category as murder!

Why does God hate pride so much? Because it is the one sin that keeps us from allowing God to use us for His purposes. When we are committed to doing things our way, we are not in a position to do things God's way. Pride renders us useless in the kingdom of God. We must always remember that God does not exist for us; we exist for Him.

The Lord will not share His glory with anyone. When we seek to take the glory for ourselves—saying, in effect, "Look at what I have accomplished! Look at me! Look at who I am!"—we deny that anything we accomplish comes about because God both enables and empowers us to accomplish it. Any good in us is by His design and redemption. Anything noteworthy that we become, we become because He wills it so. We have no goodness apart from God's goodness imparted to us.

A Bible verse that most people know is Proverbs 16:18: "Pride goes before destruction, and a haughty spirit before a fall." Not all destructions are caused by pride, but pride always ends in destruction. Usually, we lose the very thing we are the most proud about having achieved, earned, owned, or accomplished. Having pride is having too high an opinion about ourselves in relation to God and taking credit that belongs to God. Having a haughty spirit is having too high an opinion of ourselves in relation to other people and taking credit that rightfully belongs to others. Both attitudes bring about a negative consequence—adversity!

When adversity comes, it just may be the result of your prideful behavior. If so, the Lord is permitting that adversity to point out to you your pride and to encourage you to humble yourself before Him (and perhaps before other people) and to submit to His will.

What the Word Says	What the Word Says to Me
By pride comes nothing but strife (Prov. 13:10).	_____ _____
The LORD will destroy the house of the proud (Prov. 15:25).	_____ _____
A man's pride will bring him low, But the humble in spirit will retain honor (Prov. 29:23).	_____ _____ _____
For the day of the LORD of hosts Shall come upon everything proud and lofty, Upon everything lifted up— And it shall be brought low. . . . The loftiness of man shall be bowed down, And the haughtiness of men shall be brought low; The LORD alone will be exalted in that day, But the idols He shall utterly abolish (Isa. 2:12, 17–18).	_____ _____ _____ _____ _____ _____ _____ _____ _____ _____ _____ _____

2. Correcting Our Harboring of Evil

Many people are hopeful that God grades on a bell curve—the kind of grading system often used in schools where a small percentage of students receive A's and F's, a larger percentage of students receive B's and D's, and the majority of students receive C's.

The Scriptures tell us, however, that God doesn't play to averages; He is a God of absolutes. We are either evil or righteous, based upon what we have decided to do in response to Jesus Christ and His shed blood on the cross. If we accept that what Jesus did on the cross was for us and for the remission of our sins, and we receive Him as our Savior, then we move from the classification of sinner to the classification of saved.

Our salvation is a matter not of works but of a willful receiving of Jesus Christ into our lives. As long as we shut the door of our souls to Christ, we are outside God's kingdom. He still loves us. He still calls to us, and His Holy Spirit still attempts to draw us to the Father. But we are not in a position to receive the full benefits of being God's children. We are enemies of God, not heirs.

Those who hope that God will tolerate a little sinfulness are those who tend to tolerate sinfulness in themselves, to the point that they do nothing about their sin even though they recognize it as sin.

Now, you may be saying, "But we are all sinful. We all fall short of perfection." That is true. Romans 3:23 says it plainly: "All have sinned and fall short of the glory of God."

But recognizing that we are sinful should compel us to do something about it. When we see that we are sinful, we need to come to the Father and say, "I need Your forgiveness. Please wash me and make me clean in Your sight." When we recognize that we have committed a trespass against our neighbors, or that we have sinned against God, we should not brush that aside casually as if to say, "Well, that's just my human nature." Rather, we need to come to God and say, "I have sinned. Have mercy upon me. Change my human nature so I won't desire to do this again!" A recognition of evil should bring about a rebuke, a removal of evil, or a stand against evil.

Deuteronomy 19:19–20 states, "You shall put away the evil from among you. And those who remain shall hear and fear, and hereafter they shall not again commit such evil among you." Jesus told a woman who was caught in the act of blatant sin, "Go and sin no more" (John 8:3–11).

Facing the fact that we are sinful creatures is not the same as tolerating sin in our lives. The Scriptures teach us that God desires for us to hate sin and its consequences and to turn from evil at every opportunity.

We are not to imitate evil.

We are not to embrace evil.

We are not to flirt with evil.

We are not to be curious about evil.

Rather, we are to turn our backs on it and run from it at full speed.

Why does God want you to flee from evil? Because He wants to protect you from sin's consequences. The Lord can look into the future and see what you will reap when you sow sinfulness. You must recognize that you never receive only what you sow as a seed of sin. That seed produces a harvest of sinful consequences—anguish, trials, heartaches, adversity. You will receive from your sinful deed a negative consequence with interest. Sinful seed multiplies just as good seed multiplies.

Furthermore, sin *always* has negative consequences. Sin always bears its fruit. These are sobering verses of Scripture:

> *He will punish your iniquity,*
> *O daughter of Edom;*
> *He will uncover your sins! (Lam. 4:22).*

> *O God, You have cast us off;*
> *You have broken us down;*
> *You have been displeased;*
> *Oh, restore us again! (Ps. 60:1).*

> *The LORD has done what He purposed;*
> *He has fulfilled His word*
> *Which He commanded in days of old.*
> *He has thrown down and has not pitied,*
> *And He has caused an enemy to rejoice over you;*
> *He has exalted the horn of your adversaries*
> *(Lam. 2:17).*

The only antidote for sin is God's forgiveness. You can't work your way out of it or ever compensate for sin by good deeds. Only the shed blood of Jesus brings full remission of sins. The good news is that when we confess our sins to the Father, "He is faithful and just to forgive us our sins and to cleanse us from all unrighteousness" (1 John 1:9).

Another reason that God hates sin and desires for us to hate it, too, is this: God sees that sin will rob us of a future blessing. When a weed occupies a bit of ground, it keeps a fruitful plant from occupying that portion of the earth. The same goes for sin in our lives. As long as we give a safe harbor to sin, we keep ships laden with God's blessing from docking.

When adversity hits your life, face the possibility that you may not have purged all evil from your life. Ask the Lord to give you the courage and ability to change your ways, remove yourself from evil, and live a righteous life. It is possible. The Holy Spirit will enable you to do so if you ask for His help.

What the Word Says	What the Word Says to Me
Who can understand his errors?	_____
Cleanse me from secret faults.	_____
Keep back Your servant also	_____
from presumptuous sins;	_____
Let them not have dominion	_____
over me.	_____
Then I shall be blameless,	_____
And I shall be innocent of great	_____
transgression.	_____
Let the words of my mouth and	_____
the meditation of my heart	_____
Be acceptable in Your sight,	_____
O LORD, my strength and my Re-	_____
deemer (Ps. 19:12–14).	_____
He who covers his sins will not	_____

prosper,
But whoever confesses and for-
sakes them will have mercy
(Prov. 28:13).

Whoever commits sin also commits lawlessness, and sin is lawlessness. And you know that He
was manifested to take away our
sins, and in Him there is no sin.
Whoever abides in Him does not
sin. Whoever sins has neither
seen Him nor known Him
(1 John 3:4–6).

3. Correcting Our Associations

Adversity often brings us face-to-face with the fact that we need to associate with different people. Perhaps we need new friends. Perhaps we need to sever ties with certain people. Perhaps we need to align ourselves more closely with Christian believers.

We human beings were made for fellowship and communication with other human beings and with God. None of us were designed to go it alone. We need other people, and they need us.

But at times, we are unwise in the associations we make. We choose the wrong friends or employer or partner or employee. And inevitably, the bad choice brings us adversity.

The Scriptures provide a very good model for true friendship in the lives of David and Jonathan. Jonathan's love for his friend David caused him to manifest these behaviors:

- He warned his friend of possible danger (1 Sam. 19:1–3).
- He spoke well of David, even to a person who considered David to be an enemy and who was angry with Jonathan for having David as a friend (1 Sam. 19:4).

- He sought to do what David needed him to do (1 Sam. 20:4).
- He risked his life in defending David (1 Sam. 20:32–33).
- He helped David to escape death (1 Sam. 20:35–41).

One of the greatest statements of friendship in the Bible was voiced by Jonathan when he said to David, "Go in peace, since we have both sworn in the name of the LORD, saying, 'May the LORD be between you and me, and between your descendants and my descendants, forever'" (1 Sam. 20:42). Now that's friendship!

Paul described Christian friendship in a chapter of the Bible that we have come to call the love chapter, 1 Corinthians 13. He described Christian love in these ways:

Patient (v. 4)	Positive (v. 5)
Kind (v. 4)	Magnanimous (v. 6)
Humble (v. 4)	Rooted in truth (v. 6)
Polite (v. 5)	Supportive (v. 7)
Selfless (v. 5)	Hopeful (v. 7)
Unruffled (v. 5)	Enduring (v. 7)

Such love, Paul said, never fails. And such friendships do not create adversity. They are blessings in our lives, God's rich rewards to us on this earth.

Bad associations, however, bring calamity. This type of relationship is also described in Scripture. Consider the words of Deuteronomy 13:5:

> But that prophet or that dreamer of dreams shall be put to death, because he has spoken in order to turn you away from the LORD your God, who brought you out of the land of Egypt and redeemed you from the house of bondage, to entice you from the way in which the LORD your God commanded you to walk. So you shall put away the evil from your midst.

Evil associates attempt to turn us away from the Lord and His commandments. They are the friends, neighbors, relatives, or colleagues who say to us, "God didn't really say that," "God didn't really mean that," or "God won't punish a person for doing that." Some go as far as to say to us, "You're special. God won't require you to abstain from that." All of these lies are as old as the lie the serpent told in the Garden of Eden. We are to put away such friends from our lives and seek instead friends who truly love us and desire to help us walk in God's ways.

When adversity comes, you may need to look only as far as your associations to see the cause.

There is a second lesson about friends in times of adversity. True friends will stick with you in adversity, and they will stick with you all the way through your adversity until God brings you to a better and more perfect place in your life. Such a friend is one who "sticks closer than a brother" (Prov. 18:24).

Proverbs 17:17 declares, "A friend loves at all times, and a brother is born for adversity." A true friend will be there for you when you need her.

What the Word Says	What the Word Says to Me
Make no friendship with an angry man (Prov. 22:24).	_____ _____
A man who has friends must himself be friendly (Prov. 18:24).	_____ _____
He has removed my brothers far from me, And my acquaintances are completely estranged from me. My relatives have failed, And my close friends have forgotten me. Those who dwell in my house,	_____ _____ _____ _____ _____ _____ _____

and my maidservants,
Count me as a stranger;
I am an alien in their sight.
I call my servant, but he gives no
answer;
I beg him with my mouth.
My breath is offensive to my wife,
And I am repulsive to the chil-
dren of my own body.
Even young children despise me;
I arise, and they speak against me.
All my close friends abhor me,
And those whom I love have
turned against me.
My bone clings to my skin and to
my flesh,
And I have escaped by the skin
of my teeth.
Have pity on me, have pity on
me, O you my friends,
For the hand of God has struck
me!
Why do you persecute me as God
does,
And are not satisfied with my
flesh? (Job 19:13–22).

Greater love has no one than
this, than to lay down one's life
for his friends. You are My
friends if you do whatever I command you. No longer do I call
you servants, for a servant

does not know what his master
is doing; but I have called you
friends, for all things that I heard
from My Father I have made
known to you (John 15:13–15).

_____
_____
_____
_____
_____

But we command you, brethren,
in the name of our Lord Jesus
Christ, that you withdraw from
every brother who walks disor-
derly and not according to the
tradition which he received from
us (2 Thess. 3:6).

_____
_____
_____
_____
_____
_____
_____

4. Correcting Our Misplaced Priorities

Adversity nearly always corrects or adjusts our misplaced priorities. In times of adversity we are reminded of what is truly
important to us: our relationship with family and friends, our
health, our peace of mind, our ability to experience all that God
has created, and our eternal salvation and relationship with God.

Uzziah became the king over Judah at the age of sixteen. Under
the tutelage of Zechariah, Uzziah sought God, and the Bible tells
us, "As long as he sought the LORD, God made him prosper" (2
Chron. 26:5).

Uzziah accomplished great things in his reign. He defeated the
enemy Philistines, Arabians, Meunites, and Ammonites. He built
fortified towers in Jerusalem and in the desert, where he also dug
many wells. He built a strong army for the defense of Judah. His
fame spread far and wide. (See 2 Chron. 26:6–15.)

But then, Uzziah no longer sought the Lord. The Scriptures tell
us that "when he was strong his heart was lifted up, to his destruction" (2 Chron. 26:16). He attempted to supersede the priests in
the temple, and as a result, he broke out with leprosy on his
forehead, and he had leprosy until the day of his death. He dwelt

in an isolated house and was cut off from the people of God and from the house of God.

Adversity can reveal to us that we are in danger of putting other things before the Lord. Anything—or any person—that we put in the Lord's place is an idol. And the Lord gives no place to idols. He smashes them repeatedly throughout Scripture and calls them an abomination.

When adversity hits your life, the Lord may be trying to bring your priorities back into line. Ask the Lord to help you grow in an understanding of how to realign your life in a way that will bring you peace, prosperity, and blessing. Ask Him to give you the courage to drop some of your commitments or perhaps make different commitments, and to pursue the habits that lead to godly righteousness and healthy relationships.

What the Word Says	What the Word Says to Me
O God, You are my God; Early will I seek You; My soul thirsts for You; My flesh longs for You In a dry and thirsty land Where there is no water. So I have looked for You in the sanctuary, To see Your power and Your glory (Ps. 63:1–2).	_____
Seek first the kingdom of God and His righteousness, and all these things shall be added to you (Matt. 6:33).	_____
Jesus answered and said to them, "Render to Caesar the things that	_____

are Caesar's, and to God the
things that are God's" (Mark
12:17).

A Deeper Walk with the Lord

When adversity comes and the Lord leads us to self-examination that results in correction of things in our lives, He invariably pulls us into a deeper relationship with Him. A deeper look at our lives—beyond just the surface level of day-to-day living—can bring us to a deeper walk with the Lord. Old roots are subject to being unearthed and discarded. Unbelief is challenged and replaced with faith. Pride crumbles before humility.

Soldiers learn in basic training that when a group marches in formation, each person must stay true to the course established. If a soldier gets off just one degree, by the time he has marched several yards, he will be observably out of line, and if he should continue to march in error over a mile or so, he would be out of earshot of his companions. We are subject to the same error in our spiritual lives. If we begin to walk just one degree away from the truth—in pride, in harmful associations, with wrong priorities, or in concert with sin and evil—we will soon find ourselves a long way from the path of righteousness in which the Lord desires us to walk daily.

When adversity comes your way, take a look inward to see what you may need to correct in your life so that you truly stay on course with what the Lord has for you.

- *Can you recall an instance in your life in which adversity was linked to pride, a fling with sin, a bad association or friendship, or ungodly priorities? What happened?*

- *How do you feel when you know the Lord has led you into a midcourse correction for your life? How do you feel after you have made that correction?*

_____

_____

- *What insights have you gained about adversity and how to advance in your spiritual life* through *adversity?*

_____

_____

- *In what areas of your life do you feel challenged today to make corrections?*

_____

_____

LESSON 6

WHAT ADVERSITY MAY REVEAL TO US

As we discussed in the last chapter, when adversity strikes, we are wise to engage in self-examination. As we do, the Lord may lead us in a number of directions. Self-examination is not limited to areas of sinfulness or pride; it may involve areas of strength we need to pursue or in which we need to grow. Some areas worthy of examination in times of adversity are these:

- Our view of God
- The place of material possessions in our lives
- Our strengths and weaknesses
- A possible unwillingness to forgive others
- Our faith in God

We'll explore each one in this lesson. As we do, be open to what the Lord may speak to you. These are areas in which personal pride often causes us to say, "I'm all right in that area." The fact of the matter is, we can always grow in our understanding and be perfected in these areas.

Adversity Can Reveal Our View of God

When adversity hits, what is your first impression of God? Do you regard Him as a cruel taskmaster who is judging you unmercifully and requiring behavior from you that is unreasonable? Or do you regard Him as a benevolent Father who is permitting you to be chastened in a way that will result in your growth and perfection?

- *How do you feel when the Lord chastises you?*

_____

_____

The first response of many people is to feel that God is dealing with them unfairly or too harshly. If that is your response, don't deny your feelings. Instead, explore why you feel that way. In your self-examination on this point, you may discover that you have been taught incorrectly about God.

As a pastor for more than forty years, I have encountered literally hundreds of people who have a negative view of God. This opinion is usually one they have been taught by their parents, either directly or indirectly, and often it is based on a child's impression of his or her father. The Scriptures portray our heavenly Father in these terms:

- Loving (John 3:16; 1 John 4:8)
- Intimate (John 15:15)
- Patient (Ps. 103:8)
- Gentle and Gracious (Ps. 103:8)
- Generous (Luke 6:38)
- Faithful and Steadfast (Lam. 3:23)

If this is not your understanding of God, your heavenly Father, then I encourage you to look up the references next to each of the attributes above and let the Word of God speak directly to you. Reread the Gospels of Matthew, Mark, Luke, and John. Read about Jesus, who said of Himself, "He who has seen Me has seen the Father" (John 14:9). Read closely what Jesus said about the Father. Let the Holy Spirit bring healing to you in this area of your understanding about the nature of God.

At the opposite end of the spectrum, a relatively small percentage of people regard God as so loving that He would never do anything that could remotely be construed as negative toward His children. They believe that God ultimately will overlook all of their sins, as if they were of no account in His eyes. Paul wrote to the Galatians on this point, saying, "Do not be deceived, God is not mocked; for whatever a man sows, that he will also reap" (Gal. 6:7). God does not wink at sin, and neither should we. Sin is destructive and, ultimately, deadly.

The balanced view of God from Scripture is that our heavenly Father is just, righteous, and absolute, and at the same time, He is loving, generous, and available. His desire is to have warm and intimate fellowship with His children and to bless us (which is possible when we live in accordance with His laws and commandments).

Your response in adversity will reveal to you your opinion of God. Take note of your feelings and thoughts when adversity comes your way. Your understanding of the Lord and the relationship He desires to have with you may be an area in which you need to grow.

What the Word Says	What the Word Says to Me
The LORD has appeared of old to me, saying: "Yes, I have loved you with an everlasting love; Therefore with lovingkindness I have drawn you. Again I will build you, and you shall be rebuilt" (Jer. 31:3–4).	_____ _____ _____ _____ _____ _____ _____

For the LORD is righteous,
He loves righteousness;
His countenance beholds the
upright (Ps. 11:7).

The voice of the LORD breaks
the cedars,
Yes, the LORD splinters the ce-
dars of Lebanon. . . .
The voice of the LORD shakes
the wilderness. . . .
The voice of the LORD makes the
deer give birth,
And strips the forests bare;
And in His temple everyone says,
"Glory!"
The LORD sat enthroned at the
Flood,
And the LORD sits as King for-
ever.
The LORD will give strength to
His people;
The LORD will bless His people
with peace (Ps. 29:5–11).

The LORD loves justice,
And does not forsake His saints;
They are preserved forever,
But the descendants of the
wicked shall be cut off.
The righteous shall inherit the
land,
And dwell in it forever (Ps.
37:28–29).

Adversity Reveals Our Relationship to Things

When adversity strikes, one of the first things revealed to us is our materialism or lack of it. So often we hear on the news of people whose homes have been destroyed by fire, tornado, hurricane, or flood, and their first response is, "We have lost everything, but thank God, we have our lives." In the end, the things that matter to us most are our health and safety and the health and safety of loved ones. People count far more than things.

Yet, in our world, many tend to use people and value things, rather than use things and value people. We are preoccupied as a culture with acquiring material possessions—in quantities far more than what we need. We only need to take a look at the national debt, and the amount of personal debt of the citizens of our nation, and come to the conclusion that greed is rampant.

It takes adversity perhaps to call us back to our sense of values about what is truly important. The intangibles of love, hope, friendship, family togetherness, health, peace of heart, creative ideas, and an abundance of energy are far more valuable than anything we can consume or put on a shelf to admire.

What the Word Says

The cares of this world, the deceitfulness of riches, and the desires for other things entering in choke the word, and it becomes unfruitful (Mark 4:19).

Do not seek what you should eat or what you should drink, nor have an anxious mind. For all these things the nations of the world seek after, and your Father knows that you need these

What the Word Says to Me

_____

_____

_____

_____

_____

_____

_____

_____

_____

_____

things. But seek the kingdom of
God, and all these things shall be
added to you (Luke 12:29–31).

Adversity Reveals Our Strengths
and Weaknesses

When adversity strikes, we find out what we are made of. I'm
sure you have heard people say in the aftermath of a crisis or in a
long-term hardship, "Before this happened to me, I never would
have thought that I could deal with something like this."

Gideon had that type of understanding about his ability. When
the angel of the Lord came to him and said, "The LORD is with
you, you mighty man of valor!" Gideon's automatic response was,
"O my lord, if the LORD is with us, why then has all this happened
to us? And where are all His miracles? . . . The LORD has forsaken
us" (Judg. 6:12–13). Gideon saw himself and all the Israelites as
being weak and unworthy. The Lord responded to him almost as
if He hadn't heard him: "Go in this might of yours, and you shall
save Israel from the hand of the Midianites. Have I not sent you?"
(v. 14).

And again, Gideon replied with an extremely low view of
himself, "O my Lord, how can I save Israel? Indeed my clan is the
weakest in Manasseh, and I am the least in my father's house" (v.
15). And the Lord again encouraged Gideon, "Surely I will be with
you, and you shall defeat the Midianites as one man" (v. 16).

Friend, when the Lord calls you strong, don't proclaim yourself
to be weak!

When the Lord says you are forgiven, don't dwell on your past
sins!

When the Lord calls you healed, don't dredge up your past list
of ailments!

When the Lord says you are righteous, don't see yourself any
other way!

On the other hand, you err if you see yourself as powerful in
your own life to the point that you have no need of God.

Never try to cope with an adversity on your own. You need the Lord's help. Adversity brings home that lesson to us again and again. We cannot help ourselves, any more than Daniel could help himself in a den of lions or Peter could release himself from prison or Paul could save himself and his companions during a shipwreck.

The lesson, of course, is that we can't help ourselves at *any* time. We need the Lord's help every hour of every day of every year if we truly are to live our lives successfully—in spirit, mind, body, and in healthy relationships. He is our ever-present help.

We must come to the conclusion that our strength lies in the Lord and not in ourselves. As 1 Corinthians 1:25 says, "The foolishness of God is wiser than men, and the weakness of God is stronger than men." In other words, there is no comparison between God and humankind when it comes to wisdom and strength. He is infinite; we are finite. When we rely on the Lord, we have access to His unlimited power and wisdom, and therefore, we will not end up in failure. When we attempt to rely on ourselves in adversity, we usually will fail miserably and may even bring about more adversity.

What the Word Says

Seek the LORD and His strength; Seek His face evermore! (1 Chron. 16:11).

The spiritual is not first, but the natural, and afterward the spiritual. The first man was of the earth, made of dust; the second Man is the Lord from heaven. As was the man of dust, so also are those who are made of dust; and as is the heavenly Man, so also are those who are heavenly. And

What the Word Says to Me

_____

_____

_____

_____

_____

_____

_____

_____

_____

_____

_____

as we have borne the image of the
man of dust, we shall also bear
the image of the heavenly Man (1
Cor. 15:46–49).

But let all those rejoice who put
their trust in You;
Let them ever shout for joy, because You defend them (Ps. 5:11).

Then Moses and the children of
Israel sang this song to the
LORD, and spoke, saying:
"I will sing to the LORD,
For He has triumphed gloriously!
The horse and its rider
He has thrown into the sea!
The LORD is my strength and
song,
And He has become my salva-
tion;
He is my God, and I will praise
Him;
My father's God, and I will exalt
Him" (Ex. 15:1–2).

Adversity May Reveal Our
Unwillingness to Forgive

As stated in an earlier lesson, the Lord in His righteousness and
goodness can have no part in sin, and He cannot ignore sin's
presence. The Lord moves against sin continually and with the
full force of His omnipotence. Only by the mercy of God, manifest
at God's discretion, are any of us spared. Those who believe in
Jesus Christ and put themselves into a position to receive God's

forgiveness are spared the wrath of God, even though they may be the beneficiaries of the Lord's chastisement and discipline.

Those who receive forgiveness from God are expected to extend forgiveness to others. And those who extend forgiveness to others are in a position to receive God's forgiveness. Jesus said,

> Whenever you stand praying, if you have anything against anyone, forgive him, that your Father in heaven may also forgive you your trespasses. But if you do not forgive, neither will your Father in heaven forgive your trespasses (Mark 11:25–26).

Adversity sometimes reveals to us that we have not forgiven others, and therefore, we must stand in our own sin and are subject to its consequences, which are never pleasant.

Jesus told a parable to teach this lesson:

> There was a certain rich man who had a steward, and an accusation was brought to him that this man was wasting his goods. So he called him and said to him, "What is this I hear about you? Give an account of your stewardship, for you can no longer be steward." Then the steward said within himself, "What shall I do? For my master is taking the stewardship away from me. I cannot dig; I am ashamed to beg. I have resolved what to do, that when I am put out of the stewardship, they may receive me into their houses." So he called every one of his master's debtors to him, and said to the first, "How much do you owe my master?" And he said, "A hundred measures of oil." So he said to him, "Take your bill, and sit down quickly and write fifty." Then he said to another, "And how much do you owe?" So he said, "A hundred measures of wheat." And he said to him, "Take your bill, and write eighty." So the master commended the unjust steward because he had dealt shrewdly. For the sons of this world are more shrewd in their generation than the sons of light (Luke 16:1–8).

Jesus called this steward unjust, which he certainly was in his cheating and stealing from his master, but He also noted that the master commended him for his shrewdness. And what did the servant do that was so shrewd? He forgave the debts of others to his own advantage.

The Lord calls us to like behavior—*not* to the poor stewardship, but to a willing forgiveness of others. When we forgive those who may have wronged us, we are in an advantageous position to receive forgiveness from the Father.

To fail to forgive is to harbor resentment, which can grow into bitterness, which in turn always brings us into adverse relationships with others. To fail to forgive is also to harbor a desire for revenge—to make certain that the person who has wronged us is punished according to our standards of what is right and wrong, or according to our standards of what is a fair punishment. The Scriptures teach that we are to leave vengeance to the Lord and not take it upon ourselves (Rom. 12:19). Anytime we attempt to act as the judge, jury, and law for another person, we are in danger of being judged ourselves.

When you experience adversity, ask the Lord to reveal to you whether you are in a state of unforgiveness toward someone. If you are, forgive that person and seek to make restitution. Then ask the Lord to forgive you and free you from any consequences of your unforgiveness.

What the Word Says

What the Word Says to Me

Judge not, and you shall not be judged. Condemn not, and you shall not be condemned. Forgive, and you will be forgiven (Luke 6:37).

_____

_____

_____

_____

_____

If My people who are called by My name will humble themselves, and pray and seek My face, and turn from their wicked

_____

_____

_____

_____

ways, then I will hear from
heaven, and will forgive their sin
and heal their land (2 Chron.
7:14).

You ought rather to forgive and
comfort him, lest perhaps such a
one be swallowed up with too
much sorrow. Therefore I urge
you to reaffirm your love to him.
. . . Now whom you forgive anything, I also forgive. For if indeed I have forgiven anything, I
have forgiven that one for your
sakes in the presence of Christ,
lest Satan should take advantage
of us; for we are not ignorant of
his devices (2 Cor. 2:7–11).

If anyone has a complaint against
another; even as Christ forgave
you, so you also must do (Col.
3:13).

Adversity Reveals Our Faith Level

When hardships and trials come our way, we are wise to analyze
the state of our faith in God. Is our first response, "God, I trust
You to bring me through this and to work this to my eternal good,"
or is it, "Oh, my, I'm doomed and there is nothing anybody can
do"?

Could it be that the storm on the Sea of Galilee was for this
precise lesson in the lives of Jesus' disciples? Jesus said to His
disciples, "Let us cross over to the other side" (Mark 4:35). The
disciples should have taken that statement as a sure sign that Jesus

expected to arrive safe and well on the other side of the shore. But then a great windstorm arose. The waves began to beat against the boat, and the boat began to take on water and was in apparent danger of capsizing. Jesus was asleep on a pillow in the stern of the boat, oblivious to the storm in His faith that God had called Him to the other side of the lake and would ensure His safe arrival there. The disciples awoke Jesus in their fear and said, "Teacher, do You not care that we are perishing?"

How many times have we said the same thing to the Lord in our adversity? "Don't You care, Lord, that this is happening to me? Don't You love me enough, Lord, to do something about this hardship or trouble I am experiencing?"

Jesus arose and rebuked the wind and said to the sea, "Peace, be still!" And the wind ceased and there was a great calm. Then He turned to His disciples and said, "Why are you so fearful? How is it that you have no faith?" (Mark 4:40).

God has given to each one of us a measure of faith (Rom. 12:3), and He expects us to use our faith to overcome our fear. Why is this important? Because fear is always a component of adversity. A degree of fear is part of what makes a situation an adversity instead of just another experience. Fear is part of the negative dimension of an adversity.

What do we fear? Usually, an irreversible loss of some sort. We may fear a loss of life, limb, or sanity. Or in most cases, we probably fear things that are more subtle: loss of reputation, loss of status, loss of opportunity, loss of a valued relationship. Fear causes us to project the very worst that can happen—that we will never recover, that all hope is lost, and that we will never have, enjoy, or experience something again.

Faith tells the opposite story. Faith says that God is in control, and when He is in control, all things work together for our good (Rom. 8:28). Faith says that we will recover and that our final state will be better than anything we have experienced or been thus far. Faith says that whatever Satan steals from us, he must restore, and in virtually all cases, he must restore more than what he stole.

Adversity may call your faith into question, but above all, it calls your faith to action. Adversity reveals to you areas in which your faith is weak and needs to grow. Adversity reveals to you areas in which you need to act in faith and not fear. When hard times come, say to yourself, "Now is the time to use my faith in a new way." The more you use your faith, the greater it grows.

What the Word Says	What the Word Says to Me
Examine yourselves as to whether you are in the faith. Test yourselves. Do you not know yourselves, that Jesus Christ is in you? (2 Cor. 13:5).	_____ _____ _____ _____ _____
The testing of your faith produces patience. But let patience have its perfect work, that you may be perfect and complete, lacking nothing. If any of you lacks wisdom, let him ask of God, who gives to all liberally and without reproach, and it will be given to him. But let him ask in faith, with no doubting, for he who doubts is like a wave of the sea driven and tossed by the wind. For let not that man suppose that he will receive anything from the Lord; he is a double-minded man, unstable in all his ways (James 1:3–8).	_____ _____ _____ _____ _____ _____ _____ _____ _____ _____ _____ _____ _____ _____ _____ _____
In this you greatly rejoice, though now for a little while, if need be, you have been grieved by various trials, that the	_____ _____ _____ _____

genuineness of your faith, being
much more precious than gold
that perishes, though it is tested
by fire, may be found to praise,
honor, and glory at the revelation
of Jesus Christ (1 Peter 1:6–7).

_____
_____
_____
_____
_____
_____

Important Revelations for Our Growth

Each of the areas discussed in this lesson—our view of God, a reevaluation of our attitude toward material things, an appraisal of our strengths and weaknesses, an awareness of an unwillingness to forgive, and a look at our faith—is important to our spiritual growth.

It is only as we examine ourselves and reevaluate our view of God that we can begin to grow in our understanding of God's vast love and righteousness and, out of that understanding, to grasp more fully the relationship that God desires to have with us.

It is only as we confront our materialism that we can shift our priorities to things that are eternal.

It is through a study of our strengths and weaknesses that we see more clearly who the Lord created us to be in Him, and we understand with greater depth how the Lord desires to work through us.

It is when we face our unwillingness to forgive that we free ourselves from the consequences of our state of unforgiveness.

It is when we come face-to-face with the true nature of our faith level that we can begin to conquer our fears and to develop our faith.

Adversity acts in our lives as a mirror of sorts. It reveals the areas in which we need to improve, from God's viewpoint. What a benefit there is for us to gain!

Never waste an adversity. Learn all you can from each one. Truly, you can advance when you are willing to examine more closely the attributes in your life that are revealed in hard times.

- *What new insights do you have about the role that adversity might play in God's desire to perfect you?*

  _____

  _____

- *Can you recall an experience in your life in which adversity caused you to reexamine your view of God, your materialism, your weaknesses and strengths, an issue of unforgiveness, or your faith (or lack of it)?*

  _____

  _____

- *What area of your life do you believe the Lord may be challenging you to confront right now?*

  _____

  _____

LESSONS PAUL LEARNED FROM ADVERSITY

The adversity of the apostle Paul was mentioned earlier, but in this lesson, I want to explore more fully what Paul encountered and what he learned from his "thorn in the flesh." Although we are not told specifically what Paul experienced, the word for "thorn" in the passage refers to a sharp, pointed stake, not a little garden thistle or "sticker." Paul endured intense pain and suffering.

Furthermore, Paul said that the thorn was "a messenger of Satan to buffet me" (2 Cor. 12:7). The Greek word translated "buffet" is the same word (rendered "beat") used to describe the ordeal that Jesus went through in Mark 14:65 where we read, "Then some began to spit on Him, and to blindfold Him, and to beat Him, and to say to Him, 'Prophesy!' And the officers struck Him with the palms of their hands." Paul's thorn in the flesh included unrelenting anguish, one that was of a beating or pummeling variety.

Adversity comes in many packages and in varying degrees, but of one thing we can always be certain. The person who is experiencing adversity feels pain and, at times, great pain—perhaps not in an outer, visible way, but always in an inner, emotional, mental, or spiritual way.

Paul's description of his experience reveals some principles about adversity that we can apply to our lives:

- Praying for deliverance
- Recognizing we are not alone in our adversity
- Trusting God even when He doesn't remove the adversity
- Relying on God's power as sufficient to carry us through

A Prayer for Deliverance

Paul asked the Lord to deliver him from his adversity. Even though Paul recognized that the Lord had permitted him to experience the thorn in the flesh for a good reason—so that Paul would not be exalted above measure—Paul still pleaded with the Lord to free him from his pain. The Scriptures never scold us for praying for release from adversity. Jesus asked for release or a way out of an agonizing death even as He prayed in the Garden of Gethsemane (Matt. 26:39).

We are wise to pray and ask our heavenly Father to release us from the anguish of adversity. Such a prayer is not wishful thinking. It is a statement of faith that we know God can release us, and that He, indeed, will release us from our anguish. Although our release may not be immediate, we can trust with certainty that the Lord will answer our prayer in His way and in His timing.

- *How do you feel about asking the Lord to release you from heartache, pain, or adversity? Do you believe God will answer your prayer?*

Never Alone in Adversity

Paul recognized that he was not alone in his adversity. He turned to the Lord and heard from Him, "My grace is sufficient for you, for My strength is made perfect in weakness" (2 Cor. 12:9). Paul had a keen awareness that the Lord was with him in what he was experiencing.

What a comfort it is to know that the Lord is with you, and that He will never leave you! God's promise to His people through the ages has been, "I will not leave you nor forsake you" (Josh. 1:5; Heb. 13:5). Jesus promised His disciples, "Lo, I am with you always, even to the end of the age" (Matt. 28:20). No matter what you may be going through today, the Lord is with you. He will not abandon you in your troubles, even though you may feel the Lord is silent.

Often we are frustrated when we are going through adversity and the Lord doesn't choose to speak to us as He did to Paul. We may find ourselves saying, "Where is God?" We must be aware that although God may not be speaking to us, He is with us. Silence is not to be equated with inactivity. God is moving behind the scenes in ways we cannot fathom or know with our senses.

When God is silent, we have only one reasonable option—to trust Him, wait on Him, and believe that He is at work on our behalf. God may be quiet, but He has not quit on us.

- *How do you feel about the statement "God is with you in adversity"?*

When God Doesn't Remove Adversity

Paul had to face the fact that God was not going to remove the adversity. At no time did Paul make a claim that God was going to heal him, deliver him, or help him to escape fully the thorn in the flesh. The Lord made it plain to Paul that He heard Paul plead three times for release, but the Lord was not going to give him either release or relief. Rather, He was going to give him peace.

What a difficult realization that must have been for Paul! He was a man of great faith, a man who brought deliverance and healing to many, a man obviously beloved by God and by believers throughout the Greek world, and God was not going to release him from an obviously painful affliction.

Many fine Christian people experience a situation like this when a physician tells them that a disease is terminal or when they realize that a relationship is not going to be reconciled as they had hoped. To a lesser extent, although no less painful to the people involved, are situations when they realize that God has answered the prayer with a "no" answer. Discouragement and despair can set in.

We need to remember the Lord's words to Paul: "My grace is sufficient for you." The Lord may not remove our problem, but He is going to compensate fully for it. In whatever ways we are weak, He is going to be strong. He will fill in the crevices of our pain, lack of ability, heartache, and discouragement with His presence. What we aren't, He will be. What we can't do, He will do.

We must recognize that the Lord says His grace *is* sufficient—not *was* sufficient, not *will be* sufficient. Trusting God is a moment-by-moment, day-by-day experience. As we trust God, He imparts His grace. What He did for Paul, He will do for you and me.

The psalmist said, "God is our refuge and strength, a very present help in trouble" (Ps. 46:1). A "very present help" does not mean that God will act immediately to eliminate the cause of our trouble; it means that the Lord is "very present" to help us. He is intimately connected to us and, therefore, is inseparably linked to our problem. He is present!

In that same psalm, the psalmist went on to say that because God is our refuge, strength, and very present help,

> *Therefore we will not fear,*
> *Even though the earth be removed,*

And though the mountains be carried into the midst of the sea;
Though its waters roar and be troubled,
Though the mountains shake with its swelling (vv. 2–3).

Most people who experience an earthquake or violent storm at sea have moments of terror. And yet, the psalmist declares that when we know with a certainty in our hearts that God is with us in our trouble, and that He will never abandon us no matter how fierce the storm rages or how much our lives are shaken, we can have great peace of heart and mind. Our confidence is in the fact that the Lord of hosts is with us (Ps. 46:7).

- *Have you ever had a time in your life when you realized that the Lord was not going to deliver you from the anguish of a problem, but He was going to walk with you through the problem? How did that make you feel? What was the outcome?*

_____

_____

God's Nature Is Revealed Through Us

Finally, Paul discovered through his experience with a thorn in the flesh that God's power reaches its peak at the lowest point of adversity. He wrote, "Therefore I take pleasure in infirmities, in reproaches, in needs, in persecutions, in distresses, for Christ's sake. For when I am weak, then I am strong" (2 Cor. 12:10).

What a powerful statement! Paul was saying that he learned through the experience that when he allowed the grace of the Lord to be sufficient in his weakness, he was actually stronger as a result.

Consider for a moment a person who tinkers with the engine of an old car, gives up, and finally sells his "bucket of bolts" to a master mechanic. The master mechanic pulls the old engine and replaces it with a completely rebuilt one, which gives great speed and power to the old car. Those who see the vehicle on the streets—with its out-of-date, nearly antique chassis—say, "Who would have thought that an old worn-out car like that could have such zip?" Well, it's not the chassis that changed but the source of power under the hood.

That was what Paul was saying about his life. The weaker he was, the more he was energized by God's presence and power, and therefore, the stronger he was.

There is no pleasure to be derived from infirmities, reproaches, needs, persecutions, or distresses unless this is the case. But if we believe that God's grace is manifested even more in our lives the deeper our pain or the greater our adversity, then we can take joy in that fact.

I feel very confident that any person who has been through an adversity with this perspective will tell you that the spiritual blessings received from the Lord during a time of adversity far overshadowed the pain caused by the adversity itself. The pain caused by adversity—whether rooted in material or relational loss, whether physical or emotional in nature—is limited. It may seem all-encompassing, but it is limited in both scope and time. The spiritual blessings that the Lord offers are unlimited. They surpass all understanding and extend beyond time into eternity.

If the Lord does not choose to remove adversity from you, He will enable you to live with it triumphantly, victoriously, and with an inner peace that is beyond reason. The greater the adversity, the more intense the pain, or the more difficult the circumstances, the greater the glory of the Lord shines through.

- *Can you look back on an experience of adversity in your life and say, "I am grateful for that experience because I truly discovered the power of God in a new and deeper way"?*

Paul said with boldness to the Corinthians that he gladly boasted of his infirmities because it was in them that "the power of Christ" rested upon him (2 Cor. 12:9). Paul was not remotely ashamed that he had a thorn in the flesh. He was not embarrassed that the Lord had not chosen to deliver him from it. He did not hide his infirmity from the Corinthians. And at the same time, he didn't boast about his infirmities to get their sympathy or to make them think he was special in some way. Paul continually pointed toward Christ, who made his infirmity bearable and, beyond that, made his infirmity a part of his witness.

We are wise to follow Paul's example. Our weaknesses are not something about which we should be ashamed. Neither are they something about which we should lay claim as if to say, "I'm disadvantaged in this way so the Lord *has* to take care of me." Rather, our witness is this: "Just look what the Lord can do! Here I am, in dire straits (or in great turmoil or pain), and see how good and how great God is!"

In recent years, I've experienced some of the most painful moments of my life personally. At the same time, God has blessed the In Touch ministry in ways that are almost beyond my comprehension. In the natural world, a person would say, "That can't be. A leader needs to be strong and powerful in all areas of his life in order for the organization he leads to grow and excel." I give witness to the contrary. In my hours of greatest weakness, God has shown Himself to be strong. He is accomplishing what He wants to accomplish, not because of *my* strength, but because I have allowed *His* strength to fill my weakness. To God be the glory, great things He has done!

What God did for Paul, what the Lord has done for me, I believe the Lord will do for you when you experience personal adversity that threatens to level you on the inside. He will raise you up, by His power and in His power.

The verses below relate in various ways to the lessons Paul learned through his thorn-in-the-flesh experience. Note as you read that they are all passages written by Paul, a man who was no stranger to affliction and trouble. Consider how these verses about God's sufficiency relate to your life and the adversity you might have experienced, or may be experiencing right now.

What the Word Says

But God, who is rich in mercy,
because of His great love with
which He loved us, even when
we were dead in trespasses, made
us alive together with Christ (by
grace you have been saved), and
raised us up together, and made
us sit together in the heavenly
places in Christ Jesus, that in the
ages to come He might show the
exceeding riches of His grace in
His kindness toward us in Christ
Jesus (Eph. 2:4–7).

I have learned in whatever state I
am, to be content: I know how to
be abased, and I know how to
abound. Everywhere and in all
things I have learned both to be
full and to be hungry, both to
abound and to suffer need. I can
do all things through Christ who
strengthens me (Phil. 4:11–13).

Thanks be to God, who gives us
the victory through our Lord
Jesus Christ. Therefore, my beloved brethren, be steadfast, im-
movable, always abounding in
the work of the Lord, knowing
that your labor is not in vain in
the Lord (1 Cor. 15:57–58).

What the Word Says to Me

_____
_____
_____
_____
_____
_____
_____
_____
_____
_____
_____
_____

_____
_____
_____
_____
_____
_____
_____
_____
_____

_____
_____
_____
_____
_____
_____
_____

For this reason I bow my knees
to the Father of our Lord Jesus
Christ . . . that He would grant
you, according to the riches of
His glory, to be strengthened
with might through His Spirit in
the inner man, that Christ may
dwell in your hearts through
faith . . . that you may be filled
with all the fullness of God. Now
to Him who is able to do exceed-
ingly abundantly above all that
we ask or think, according to the
power that works in us, to Him
be glory in the church by Christ
Jesus to all generations, forever
and ever. Amen (Eph. 3:14–20).

Set your mind on things above,
not on things on the earth (Col.
3:2).

Rejoice always, pray without ceas-
ing, in everything give thanks;
for this is the will of God in
Christ Jesus for you (1 Thess.
5:16–18).

This is a faithful saying:
For if we died with Him,
We shall also live with Him.
If we endure,
We shall also reign with Him.
If we deny Him,
He also will deny us.

If we are faithless,
He remains faithful;
He cannot deny Himself (2 Tim.
2:11–13).

But the Lord stood with me and
strengthened me, so that the message might be preached fully
through me, and that all the Gentiles might hear. Also I was delivered out of the mouth of the lion.
And the Lord will deliver me
from every evil work and preserve me for His heavenly kingdom. To Him be glory forever
and ever. Amen! (2 Tim. 4:17–
18).

- *What new insights have you gained about how to advance through adversity?*

  _____

  _____

"Advancing" Through Adversity

The theme of this entire study on adversity has been how we might "advance" through adversity. The questions may arise: But to what do we advance? What is the end to which we should aspire as we are going through times of anguish, heartache, or trial? In this lesson we will deal specifically with three goals that we can always have in any time of adversity. I phrase them here as prayers:

1. "Lord, purify and enlarge and prove my faith as the result of my going through this time of trouble."
2. "Lord, give me greater compassion for others, and especially for those who do not know You, as the result of this adversity."
3. "Lord, use this adversity in my life to prepare me to minister comfort, encouragement, and Your Word to others."

We can pray these prayers with confidence, knowing that they are all prayers the Lord desires to answer with a resounding yes in our lives!

Advancing to Greater and Purer Faith

Have you ever seen a precious metal in the process of refinement? The metal—such as gold or silver—is heated to extremely high temperatures so that the metal becomes liquid. Anything that is an impurity, or dross, floats to the top of the cauldron in which the metal is contained. The dross is skimmed away, leaving the metal pure and nearly translucent in its appearance. Only when the metal is pure is it poured into molds where it cools and becomes bullion, rare and precious.

The Lord uses adversity in a similar way in our lives to purify our faith. The Lord desires that we have both a perfect and a proven faith.

Faith can be viewed in two ways—by quantity and by quality.

In various references in the Scriptures, faith is described by quantity as being little, great, or perfect. Little faith says, "God can do it, but He may not." Great faith says, "God can do it and He will do it." Perfect faith says, "God said He'd do it so it's done." When we have perfect faith, we have absolutely no doubt that God is God in every moment and in every circumstance of our lives. We are truly living by His Word, trusting God to fulfill every detail of His Word in our personal lives.

Faith also has three types of quality: inherited, textbook, and proven.

Inherited faith is faith we may have received from a parent or a pastor. We believe that faith works because we have seen it work in the lives of others. We believe in Christ Jesus because others have believed. We acknowledge God's Word as real and potent because we have seen it lived out and working in the lives of those we trust. Paul reminded Timothy that Timothy's faith "dwelt first in your grandmother Lois and your mother Eunice" (2 Tim. 1:5). Timothy had grown up in the faith.

Textbook faith is Bible book faith. It is faith that is mostly mental. We read what the Bible says and we declare, "I believe that is true. What the Bible says is the truth of God for humankind." We believe the stories we read in the Bible; we believe that Paul and others are telling us the truth in the letters that are part of the

New Testament; we believe in God because, as the old gospel song says, "the Bible tells us so."

Both inherited faith and textbook faith are good and important to have. We benefit greatly from growing up in families in which a love of God is nourished and the Bible is taught. We grow in faith from reading the Word of God and hearing sermons based on the Bible. But the third type of faith, proven faith, is the most important.

Proven faith is faith that we have because we have tested the principles of the Bible for ourselves in times of adversity. This is the type of faith described in 1 Peter 1:6–7: "Now for a little while . . . you have been grieved by various trials, that the genuineness of your faith . . . may be found to praise, honor, and glory at the revelation of Jesus Christ."

When we use our faith in times of adversity, we can trust God to give us greater faith; in other words, to grow our faith toward perfect faith. And we can be assured that we are acquiring proven faith.

Elijah had a proven faith in God. When God sent him to the Brook Cherith, Elijah obeyed. And there by the brook, the Lord fed Elijah with bread and meat brought to him by ravens. No doubt Elijah came to count on the birds to show up in the morning and the evening with his daily ration from God. Elijah had his needs met, with sufficient food to eat and water to drink.

And then the brook dried up. The word of the Lord came again to Elijah, "Arise, go to Zarephath." And Elijah obeyed. There in Zarephath a widow made a cake for him from her last oil and flour, and God provided a miracle so that her jar of oil and bin of flour did not run out. She continued to feed herself, her son, and Elijah from the unending source until the famine ended and food was available once again. Elijah, who had experienced in his faith walk the provision of the Lord, was able to proclaim to the widow the word that God was going to provide for her, regardless of what her circumstances told her. That's faith—knowing that God is going to fulfill His Word and care for His children, regardless of the severity of a situation. (See 1 Kings 17.)

How does adversity purify our faith? First, our faith is valuable not because we possess faith, but because of Christ Jesus, who is the object of our faith. The object of our faith defines our faith. He is pure, and the quality that He gives to our faith is purity.

Second, adversity strips away from us everything but Christ. In times of adversity we realize that nothing else satisfies but Jesus Christ, and nothing is secure except Christ's presence in our lives. The money in which we trust may be lost in bankruptcy. The friends in which we placed our faith may desert us or die. The house in which we felt secure may go up in flames. The relationship on which we based our identity may end in some form of estrangement. When all has been stripped away by adversity, we see clearly that Jesus Christ remains. He alone is utterly and eternally steadfast.

Proven faith is faith that endures because it is based on our personal knowledge and experience that God endures.

God desires for us to have a pure, perfect, and proven faith, and therefore, He will answer yes when we pray, "Lord, purify and enlarge and prove my faith as the result of my going through this time of trouble."

What the Word Says	What the Word Says to Me
When I cry out to You, Then my enemies will turn back; This I know, because God is for me. In God (I will praise His word), In the LORD (I will praise His word), In God I have put my trust; I will not be afraid. What can man do to me? (Ps. 56:9–11).	_____ _____ _____ _____ _____ _____ _____ _____ _____
Let us lay aside every weight, and the sin which so easily ensnares us, and let us run with	_____ _____ _____

endurance the race that is set before us, looking unto Jesus, the
author and finisher of our faith
(Heb. 12:1–2).

Be sober, be vigilant; because
your adversary the devil walks
about like a roaring lion, seeking
whom he may devour. Resist
him, steadfast in the faith, knowing that the same sufferings are
experienced by your brotherhood
in the world. But may the God of
all grace . . . perfect, establish,
strengthen, and settle you (1 Peter 5:8–10).

- *Reflect upon an experience of hardship or heartache in your life. What was the outcome on your faith?*

_____

_____

Advancing to Greater Compassion

Adversity gives us a special kinship of spirit with other people and causes us, if we will allow it to do this work, to have a greater compassion for other people.

When we are struck with pain of a particular variety, we nearly always are amazed at how many other people have experienced that same pain—pain to which we might have been blind in the past. Many divorced people have shared with me how they never had much sympathy for or empathy with divorced people when they felt secure and happy in their marriage, but when their marriage disintegrated, they found they had much greater compassion for those who had been through a divorce or were facing the possibility of being divorced. The same goes for those with sickness. The person who has the most compassion for someone diagnosed with a life-threatening ailment is likely to be a person who currently has, or has conquered, that same disease. The mother of a child with AIDS is going to have far greater compassion for another mother in a similar circumstance than the mother of a healthy child.

We may want to have greater empathy for people in certain circumstances or situations, but the fact of the matter is that we rarely do have great empathy unless our lives have been touched by the same or a closely related problem.

Certainly, we as believers in Christ Jesus can have this empathy for those who don't know the Lord in a personal way. We have been delivered from the anguish, heartache, and adversity wrought by sin. How much more should we be able to feel for those who are still living in sin, and desire to intercede in prayer for them, reach out in love to them, and share the gospel of Christ with them!

Adversity either hardens or softens us. If we let it harden us, we are subject to more adversity. If we allow it to soften us, adversity can lead us to advance in our compassion for others.

The Lord desired that Jeremiah learn this lesson in a vivid way, and He said to him, "Arise and go down to the potter's house, and there I will cause you to hear My words." So Jeremiah went down to the potter's house, and there he found a potter making something at his wheel. The vessel he made of clay was marred in some way, so the potter crushed the clay back into the turn of the wheel and began to remake it into another vessel, one that seemed good to the potter. The word of the Lord came to Jeremiah again, saying, "O house of Israel, can I not do with you as this potter? ... Look, as the clay is in the potter's hand, so are you in My hand, O house of Israel!" (See Jer. 18:1–6.)

The same is true for our lives. The Lord desires to see some traits in us to the point that He will work and rework and rework us as clay in His hands until we manifest the traits He desires. Compassion for others is one trait. Compassion gives rise to patience, prayer, generosity, kindness, and actions rooted in love. Compassion moved Jesus to heal the people and give them words of life-giving blessing. Compassion moves us to rescue people from evil and turn them to Jesus Christ, the source of all that is good.

Let the adversity you experience work in you the good work of compassion. Have confidence that the Lord will always answer yes to the prayer, "Lord, give me greater compassion for others, especially for those who do not know You."

What the Word Says

What the Word Says to Me

Then Peter came to Him and said, "Lord, how often shall my brother sin against me, and I forgive him? Up to seven times?" Jesus said to him, "I do not say to you, up to seven times, but up to seventy times seven. Therefore the kingdom of heaven is like a certain king who wanted to settle accounts with his servants. And when he had begun to settle accounts, one was brought to him who owed him ten thousand talents. But as he was not able to pay, his master commanded that he be sold, with his wife and children and all that he had, and that payment be made. The servant therefore fell down before him, saying, 'Master, have patience with me, and I will pay you all.' Then the master of that servant

_____
_____
_____
_____
_____
_____
_____
_____
_____
_____
_____
_____
_____
_____
_____
_____
_____
_____
_____
_____
_____

was moved with compassion, re-
leased him, and forgave him the
debt. But that servant went out
and found one of his fellow servants who owed him a hundred
denarii; and he laid hands on
him and took him by the throat,
saying, 'Pay me what you owe!'
So his fellow servant fell down at
his feet and begged him, saying,
'Have patience with me, and I
will pay you all.' And he would
not, but went and threw him into
prison till he should pay the
debt. So when his fellow servants
saw what had been done, they
were very grieved, and came and
told their master all that had
been done. Then his master, after
he had called him, said to him,
'You wicked servant! I forgave
you all that debt because you
begged me. Should you not also
have had compassion on your fellow servant, just as I had pity on
you?' And his master was angry,
and delivered him to the tortur-
ers until he should pay all that
was due to him. So My heavenly
Father also will do to you if each
of you, from his heart, does not
forgive his brother his trespasses"
(Matt. 18:21–35).

All of you be of one mind, having compassion for one another; love as brothers, be tenderhearted, be courteous; not returning evil for evil or reviling for reviling, but on the contrary blessing, knowing that you were called to this, that you may inherit a blessing (1 Peter 3:8–9).

_____
_____
_____
_____
_____
_____
_____
_____

- *Reflect on your life experiences. How did you acquire compassion for certain people or groups of people?*

_____

_____

- *How do you feel when you receive compassion from others, especially in times of adversity? How do you feel when you extend compassion?*

_____

_____

Advancing to a New Dimension of Ministry

Adversity prepares us in unique ways for ministry. God wants each of us to be involved in the ministry of comforting others. But it is a very poor comforter who has never needed comfort. Adversity equips us to minister to others as nothing else can.

I readily admit that there was a time in my life when I gave very little comfort to people who were going through hard times emotionally. A big part of me believed that if people would just confess their sin, they could find peace of mind and live happily ever after. All that has changed for me in recent years. Having gone through hard times emotionally, I now can feel the hurt of a man or woman who sits in my office and cries. I can identify with those who desperately seek change in their lives but don't know where to begin. I can relate to those who are frustrated and yet are unable to pinpoint the nature of their hurts. I know better how to comfort them, even as I counsel them.

There is a difference between our ability to minister the Word of God to people and our ability to minister to people. To minister the Word of God, we need to know the Word of God and to see how it applies to various situations. But we need more than a knowledge of the Word if our ministry is to be received well by a person in need.

Truly to minister to people, we need proven faith, compassion, and an ability to empathize with people's feelings, if not their exact situation. As we have already discussed in this lesson, proven faith and compassion are derived to a great extent from adversity. Adversity prepares us to minister to people, to comfort and encourage them, and to build them up to trust God, to believe God's Word, and to expect God's best.

To comfort others is to impart strength and hope to them. By strength, of course, I mean Christ's strength. Our goal as comforters is to move people from relying on their own strength to that of Christ Jesus. Every time I read the biography of a great saint I am encouraged by God's grace to that person in times of adversity and difficulty. I come away thinking, *If God sustained that individual through such trials, He will sustain me as well*. The person's testimony imparts strength to me and motivates me to go forward rather than to give up.

To impart hope is to enable others to take their focus off their immediate circumstances and place it on eternal things. We will not completely understand much of our suffering until we see Jesus. But we have the hope that we will see Him, and that He will tie all the loose ends of our lives together in a way that makes sense. The apostle Paul described this hope in 2 Cor. 4:16–18:

> Therefore we do not lose heart. Even though our outward man is perishing, yet the inward man is being renewed day by day. For our light affliction, which is but for a moment, is working for us a far more exceeding and eternal weight

of glory, while we do not look at the things which are seen, but at the things which are not seen. For the things which are seen are temporary, but the things which are not seen are eternal.

Keep in mind that it was only after the disciples of Jesus had been through the adversity of their beloved Lord's crucifixion and resurrection—a period of intense persecution to the point that the disciples huddled in fear behind locked doors—that the Lord said to them, "Go therefore and make disciples of all the nations, baptizing them in the name of the Father and of the Son and of the Holy Spirit, teaching them to observe all things that I have commanded you; and lo, I am with you always, even to the end of the age" (Matt. 28:19–20).

When we come through adversity with stronger faith and greater compassion, we will soon find people to whom we can minister both strength and hope. In so doing, we will find an enlarged purpose for our lives and have a much deeper feeling of fulfillment and inner satisfaction that we are being used by God to fulfill His plan on the earth. The Lord always answers yes to the prayer, "Lord, use this adversity in my life to prepare me to minister comfort, encouragement, and Your Word to others."

What the Word Says

I beseech you therefore, brethren, by the mercies of God, that you present your bodies a living sacrifice, holy, acceptable to God, which is your reasonable service. . . . Let love be without hypocrisy. Abhor what is evil. Cling to what is good. Be kindly affectionate to one another with brotherly love, in honor giving preference

What the Word Says to Me

_____
_____
_____
_____
_____
_____
_____
_____
_____

to one another; not lagging in diligence, fervent in spirit, serving the Lord; rejoicing in hope, patient in tribulation, continuing steadfastly in prayer; distributing to the needs of the saints, given to hospitality. Bless those who persecute you; bless and do not curse. Rejoice with those who rejoice, and weep with those who weep. Be of the same mind toward one another. Do not set your mind on high things, but associate with the humble. Do not be wise in your own opinion. Repay no one evil for evil. Have regard for good things in the sight of all men. If it is possible, as much as depends on you, live peaceably with all men (Rom. 12:1, 9–18).

The righteous will answer Him, saying, "Lord, when did we see You hungry and feed You, or thirsty and give You drink? When did we see You a stranger and take You in, or naked and clothe You? Or when did we see You sick, or in prison, and come to You?" And the King will answer and say to them, "Assuredly, I say to you, inasmuch as you did it to one of the least of these My brethren, you did it to Me" (Matt. 25:37–40).

_____
_____
_____

- *How have your past experiences qualified you for ministry to others?*

_____

_____

Advancing to Maturity in Christ

The person who is advancing in faith toward a perfect, proven, pure faith, able to share the Word of God with others in a way that is applicable to life's needs and circumstances, the person who is advancing in compassion for others, the person who is advancing to a new level of ministry, truly able and willing to comfort those who are in trouble, sickness, or any kind of need, is a spiritually maturing Christian. Adversity compels you to grow in Christ if you only will avail yourself of the opportunity to learn and grow.

- *What new insights have you gained regarding how to advance through adversity?*

_____

_____

COURAGE IN TIMES OF ADVERSITY

In many ways, a time of adversity is like boot camp; it is rigorous, painful, and challenging. Adversity causes us to adopt new routines and habits, to develop aspects of our being—physical, mental, emotional, or spiritual—that might have been undeveloped or underdeveloped previously. Adversity sometimes puts us under the authority of people who affect our lives in ways that are foreign to us. In all these areas, we need courage to keep our balance as we feel hit by so many new feelings, facts, restrictions or limitations, obstacles and challenges, and offerings of advice and help.

Courage is required not only to face and endure times of adversity, but also to make the changes in our lives that adversity compels us to make. In either case, we can trust the Holy Spirit to help us in times of adversity and to grow and change so that we live in keeping with the example set by Jesus Christ.

Joshua knew about adversity. Certainly, forty years of wandering in a wilderness qualified him to understand hardship, trials, and troubles—physical, relational, spiritual, and no doubt emotional and mental. Joshua also knew that the Lord was with him and his people. As a close associate of Moses, Joshua had grown in his faith and leadership abilities. The time came for the people of God to cross the Jordan River and inhabit the land of promise, and Joshua was named the leader to succeed Moses.

Three times, the Lord spoke to Joshua about courage:

> Be strong and of good courage, for to this people you shall divide as an inheritance the land which I swore to their fathers to give them (Josh. 1:6).

> Only be strong and very courageous, that you may observe to do according to all the law which Moses My servant commanded you (Josh. 1:7).

> Have I not commanded you? Be strong and of good courage; do not be afraid, nor be dismayed, for the LORD your God is with you wherever you go (Josh. 1:9).

Note the three things that required courage of Joshua: (1) to make decisions that affected other people under his leadership, (2) to keep the laws and commandments, even as changes were occurring, and (3) to remember continually that the Lord was with him, the implication being in spite of what circumstances might indicate to the contrary.

We need courage in the same three areas of our lives as we face adversity.

Reaching Out to Others Takes Courage

We need God's wisdom to know how to deal with people. Our times of adversity and heartache always involve people we love. We need courage to get beyond our pain and help our children, parents, spouses, associates, and other loved ones and colleagues to cope with the pain they also are likely to be feeling. It takes tremendous inner fortitude to get beyond ourselves—to put aside our inner hurt and frustration—and to be concerned about others when we are sick, facing a loss, or in emotional turmoil. Yet, that is precisely what the Lord wants us to do. That's *why* the Lord gives us courage.

In fact, in getting outside ourselves and helping others in need we often find the strength to get through adversity. Time and again, I've watched people who were going through hard times reach out to help those who were hurting just as much as they were—although perhaps in a different way—and have seen them benefit, not from what they received from others, but from what they gave to others. This principle of God defies human reasoning, but it is absolutely true in God's kingdom.

Luke 6:38 tells us,

> Give, and it will be given to you: good measure, pressed down, shaken together, and running over will be put into your bosom. For with the same measure that you use, it will be measured back to you.

We assume that when we give, we have less than we had before. But in God's eyes, when we give, we open ourselves up to receiving in a way that results in a blessing, both materially and spiritually.

Just when you think you have nothing to give, that's the time to give! It takes courage to do so, but the Lord promises to give you that courage. Ask Him to help you, to guide you, and to show you the person or people to whom you should give. Ask Him to reveal to you the best gift possible, in the best timing and for the best results.

What the Word Says	What the Word Says to Me
Confess your trespasses to one another, and pray for one another, that you may be healed (James 5:16).	_____ _____ _____ _____

He who is greatest among you,
let him be as the younger, and he
who governs as he who serves
(Luke 22:26).

_____
_____
_____
_____

Do not be overcome by evil, but
overcome evil with good (Rom.
12:21).

_____
_____
_____

- *In what ways do you feel the Lord challenging you to have greater courage in giving to others around you?*

Keeping God's Laws Requires Courage

Adversity can knock us off stride. Often our routines or locations change in a time of adversity. A flood may force us from home; an illness may force a change in work habits. Life can be tumultuous.

We need courage to remain true to God's Word and to live according to God's commandments to us. This is especially important when we confront discouragement, disappointment, or despair in the aftermath of adversity. Our loss or pain may lead us to think, *What's the use? Why bother? Why live a godly life if this is what happens to Christians?*

Remember always that the Lord doesn't promise us success and ease in this life. He promises us His presence and His eternal rewards.

Time and again in the law of Moses we find the word *keep*. The children of Israel were commanded to keep the feasts, to keep the law and commandments, to keep the Sabbath day holy, to keep the ordinances, to keep their oaths to God, to keep themselves from evil, to keep God's judgments. To keep means to hold fast and to cherish at the same time. When adversity strikes, that should be our mind-set: above all else, we need to hold fast to the Lord and cherish our relationship with Him. Rather than blame God or turn from God, we need to turn to God and rely on His help.

Moses said to the children of Israel as he led them into a covenant relationship with God: "Therefore keep the words of this covenant, and do them, that you may prosper in all that you do" (Deut. 29:9). Keeping God's laws in the face of adversity actually leads us toward prosperity—a better state of being.

That was the advice of King David to his son Solomon. He said to Solomon as part of his final blessing to him,

> You will prosper, if you take care to fulfill the statutes and judgments with which the LORD charged Moses concerning Israel. Be strong and of good courage; do not fear nor be dismayed (1 Chron. 22:13).

When adversity hits you, those around you may criticize you for clinging to your faith or reaffirming your belief that God is a good and benevolent heavenly Father. They may mock you or scorn you. Don't be dismayed if that happens. Continue to keep God's Word and to be faithful in your relationship with the Lord. Ask the Lord to give you courage to withstand the hurtful comments of others and to be able to give a bold witness about God's power and presence even in your time of trouble.

What the Word Says	What the Word Says to Me
Whoever confesses Me before men, him I will also confess before My Father who is in heaven. But whoever denies Me before men, him I will also deny before My Father who is in heaven (Matt. 10:32–33).	_____ _____ _____ _____ _____ _____ _____

So they called them and commanded them not to speak at all nor teach in the name of Jesus. But Peter and John answered and said to them, "Whether it is right in the sight of God to listen to you more than to God, you judge. For we cannot but speak the things which we have seen and heard." . . . And being let go, they went to their own companions and reported all that the chief priests and elders had said to them. So when they heard that, they raised their voice to God . . . "Now, Lord, look on their threats, and grant to Your servants that with all boldness they may speak Your word" (Acts 4:18–20, 23–24, 29).

I would have lost heart, unless I had believed
That I would see the goodness of the LORD
In the land of the living.
Wait on the LORD;
Be of good courage,
And He shall strengthen your heart;
Wait, I say, on the LORD! (Ps. 27:13–14).

- *In what ways do you feel challenged to have greater courage in living your life according to God's laws and commandments?*

_____

_____

Courage to Hope and to Believe

In times of adversity, things can sometimes seem so bleak and so dark that we are on the verge of giving up hope. Others around us may foretell doom and encourage us to face what they see as inevitable. Job's wife was one such person. After Job was covered with painful boils from the soles of his feet to the crown of his head, she said to him, "Do you still hold fast to your integrity? Curse God and die!" (Job 2:9).

Job wisely responded to her, "You speak as one of the foolish women speaks. Shall we indeed accept good from God, and shall we not accept adversity?" (v. 10). The Scriptures add this important line: "In all this Job did not sin with his lips" (v. 10).

When you are faced with negative circumstances and then negative opinions and comments from others, you need courage to stay positive—to continue to believe that the Lord is with you! Hope and faith are not automatic responses in times of hardship and trial. They require an exercise of the will, bolstered with courage. At times, you must say aloud to yourself, "I know that God has a purpose in this. I know that God will bring me through this. I know that God is a good and loving Father, and He is doing a good and eternal work in my life." If no one else speaks hope to you, you need to speak it to yourself.

Part of the need for courage also may reside in the need to withstand the enemies who are moving against your life—in other words, those who are causing your adversity. Moses realized that would be the case for Joshua and the Israelites, and he said to the Israelites, "Be strong and of good courage, do not fear nor be afraid of them; for the LORD your God, He is the One who goes with you. He will not leave you nor forsake you" (Deut. 31:6).

It takes courage to continue to believe in God and to have hope in God's power over your enemies while your adversaries are pummeling you into the ground or threatening to do so. Goliath no doubt found David's claims about the goodness and greatness of God to be ludicrous as he stood in the Valley of Elah and watched a stick of a lad run toward him. But at the end of the day, David had victory in his hand and joy in his heart. (See 1 Sam. 17.)

Ask the Lord to give you courage to continue to believe in Him and in His presence with you as you go through adversity. Ask Him to renew your hope and faith. I have no doubt He'll honor your request.

What the Word Says	What the Word Says to Me
Oh, love the LORD, all you His saints! For the LORD preserves the faithful, And fully repays the proud person. Be of good courage, And He shall strengthen your heart, All you who hope in the LORD (Ps. 31:23–24).	_____ _____ _____ _____ _____ _____ _____ _____ _____ _____ _____
Behave courageously, and the LORD will be with the good (2 Chron. 19:11).	_____ _____ _____
It is of faith that it might be according to grace, so that the promise might be sure to all the seed, not only to those who are of the law, but also to those who are of the faith of Abraham, who is	_____ _____ _____ _____ _____ _____

the father of us all . . . who, contrary to hope, in hope believed, so that he became the father of many nations, according to what was spoken, "So shall your descendants be." And not being weak in faith, he did not consider his own body, already dead (since he was about a hundred years old), and the deadness of Sarah's womb. He did not waver at the promise of God through unbelief, but was strengthened in faith, giving glory to God, and being fully convinced that what He had promised He was also able to perform (Rom. 4:16–21).

- *In what ways do you feel challenged to ask the Lord for greater courage in trusting Him?*

_____

_____

Courage to Be Like Jesus

When we think of One who had the courage to help others in spite of intense persecution, of One who kept God's laws and commandments in spite of great temptation, of One who never stopped believing in His Father, even in His darkest hours of anguish, we must think of Jesus. Jesus was a man of courage. He trusted the Father to give Him courage, and He exercised that courage in fulfilling the Father's will for His life. He is our example.

God glorifies Himself in us and through us not simply so that we might be saved but so that we might reflect His life on this earth. He desires that we be conformed to His likeness so that when others see us helping people, declaring the truth of His Word, and trusting in Him regardless of our adversity and in spite of our adversity, they will want to know more about the love of God and the power of God in us. When we are courageous to do what the Lord both commands and empowers us to do, we truly are His witnesses because we reflect His presence in the world.

Our lives have a purpose far beyond comfort, ease, or pleasure. Our lives are intended to be used by God, to fulfill His purposes on the earth.

Take courage today, no matter what you are facing. God will give you courage when you ask Him for it. He will honor your courage in remaining true to Him and His Word, and in giving to others out of your need. A wonderful blessing is in store for the courageous!

- *What new insights have you gained about how to advance spiritually in times of adversity?*

_____

_____

LESSON 10

OUR RESPONSE TO ADVERSITY

In each lesson of this study, we have discussed ways in which we should respond to adversity, but in this lesson, I want to recap the key points in a concise, sequential way.

No one can avoid adversity completely. The winds of adversity blow in all directions. The certain fact is, we *will* have adversity in our lives.

What each of us has the power to do, however, is to choose the response to adversity. We have it within the power of our will to determine how we will face adversity and how we will behave in times of adversity.

You must realize that the most vital outcome of adversity is the formation of your character. That outcome of adversity is eternal and is most important to the heavenly Father. Material possessions may be restored, relationships may be reconciled, the body may be healed, but all of these solutions are temporary in that they are bound to this lifetime. What happens to you on the inside will count forever.

A response to adversity must be intentional. If we go with the flow, we will not grow. We may be weakened or destroyed if we respond at a superficial or an emotion-only level. Such responses are likely to be these: placing blame on others, being self-justifying, having a pity party, becoming bitter, adopting a spirit of revenge, becoming hateful or resentful, becoming disillusioned about life and God. In the end, if these patterns are not reversed, we can lose our souls because each of these behaviors leads us to turn from God and refuse to trust Him with our lives.

If we refuse to benefit from adversity, we actually choose to be destroyed by adversity. If we give in to the negative downward spiral that adversity can create, we will find that

- the adversity multiplies, growing ever more negative and painful.
- the adversity is prolonged.
- the adversity becomes more destructive, especially to our Christian witness.

The sure guarantee of all adversity that we allow to go unchecked and unmediated by the Lord is more adversity. We lose ground, rather than advance, if we fail to choose to learn and grow during life's toughest times.

When adversity hits, we must make a decision that we will, with God's help, come through our time of hardship better, not bitter. We must choose to burrow into our relationship with God rather than ignore or blame God and cast aside our faith. We must choose to do the hard work of self-examination rather than live in denial and blame others or the devil.

As we discussed in the previous chapter, this intentional approach to adversity takes courage. But this is the only way we will ever advance in our spiritual walk.

There are two major categories of response we must make to adversity: one type of response is necessary if sin is involved, another type if the adversity is a hit from Satan, permitted by God.

The Response to Adversity Caused by Sin

If in self-examination you conclude that sin is at the root of your adversity, you must take these steps:

1. *You must accept responsibility for what you have done or left undone.* Some sins are the result of your action; others are the result

of what you should have done but didn't do. Both result in negative consequences. You must acknowledge that you own part of the problem in which you find yourself.

2. *Once you have faced up to your sin, you must confess it to God.* You need to go to your heavenly Father and admit to Him that you know you have sinned, that you are truly sorry for doing so (and not merely sorry that you have been caught), and that you desire His forgiveness. No matter what you have done, you can be assured that when you ask the Lord to forgive you, He will do so. As long as you still have a conscience and an awareness that you have sinned before the Father, you are a candidate for God's forgiveness. He grants that forgiveness freely, based on the price that Jesus Christ paid on the cross for your redemption. You cannot earn God's forgiveness; you can only receive and accept it.

3. *Once you have received God's forgiveness, you must forgive yourself.* Refuse to wallow in memories of pain and self-recrimination. Make a decision to move forward in your life, with the freedom given you by God to embrace His ways and His righteousness.

Part of your move forward may involve making amends or seeking reconciliation with another person. If so, take action quickly. Once you have asked forgiveness of another person, made amends, or been reconciled, refuse to live in the past or to dredge up your past sin in future conversations or dealings with that person. Live a new life before the person you wronged or were associated with in your sin. Adopt a new way of relating to that person so that both of you live in righteousness.

If the other person rejects your request for forgiveness, or refuses to live according to God's plan, recognize that before God, you have done all that He requires you to do. Move forward and refuse to be held back by another person's disobedience to the Father.

4. *In moving forward, you must choose God's will for your life.* This is at the heart of repentance, which literally means to turn around as an act of your will. You must make new decisions to live in a way that is pleasing to God, and not in the way that was a part of your past sin—and then follow through on the decisions.

5. *As you move forward with God's grace and by the power of the Holy*

Spirit working in you, choose to respond positively to your adversity. Refuse to give in to complaining or whining about your adversity. Choose instead to respond positively to your adversity by

- taking a long, hard look at your life and searching out ways in which you may become stronger and more positive (especially in areas where you have been weak or negative in your thinking).
- accepting your adversity as a lesson from God intended to teach you what *not* to do in the future.
- thanking God that He has loved you enough not to allow you to get by with your sin and, thus, eventually to face even more dire circumstances (including everlasting punishment).

When you respond to sin-related adversity in these ways, you probably feel cleaner, stronger, and better than you have ever felt before! You have great freedom in your spirit and joy in your step. Indeed, you have *advanced* in your spiritual walk.

If you do not feel this way after confessing your sin to God, making amends, and moving forward in your life, reassess which of these five steps you might not have completed.

- *Have you ever had an experience in which you knew that sin was at the root of your adversity? How did you respond? What was the outcome?*

_____

- *How do you feel when you recognize that you have sinned? How do you feel after you confess your sin to God and receive His forgiveness?*

_____

- *How do you feel when others come to you asking for forgiveness?*

How do you feel after you have asked forgiveness of others and have been granted it?

_____

_____

- *Have you ever asked forgiveness of another person and not received it? What did you do? What was the outcome?*

_____

_____

- *What new insights do you have about how to advance beyond sin-related adversity?*

_____

_____

The Response to Adversity Permitted by God

Whether we think that our adversity is caused by Satan or caused by God, our response to it is the same. Why? Because we are believers in Christ Jesus, no adversity from Satan can come into our lives apart from God's allowing it.

If you are not a believer in Christ Jesus, then you must deal with the adversity as if it is a consequence of your sin, or you must seek to establish a relationship with your heavenly Father so you will have the full benefit of His help in your crisis. God might have allowed adversity in your life for this precise purpose: that you might turn to Him and place your trust in Jesus Christ as your Savior. In this case, you should refer to the section above. Your ownership of the problem may be that you are a sinful person living in a fallen world. This is the only explanation necessary, for example, in cases of natural catastrophes.

If you are a believer in Christ Jesus, then you need to take these steps in responding to adversity:

1. *Reaffirm your relationship with God.* You may want to review the steps listed in the section above as a reinforcement to your own

heart and mind that you are in right standing before the Father, and that Jesus Christ is Lord of your life.

2. *Pray for removal of the adversity.* Ask others to join with you in praying that God might deliver you from the evil besetting you. Recognize that your willingness to pray may be the very lesson that the Lord has for the adversity in your life: to get you to trust Him enough, and to activate your faith to the point that you ask Him to remove the difficult circumstances you face. Pray, "Deliver me, Lord! And give me a heart of thanksgiving for the good work You are going to do even as I wait to see it brought to light."

3. *Yield to God's timetable for removal of the adversity.* Not all adversity is reversed instantaneously, but all adversity is reversed inevitably. Be patient and allow God to do His full work in your life and the lives of others who may be involved. Don't rush to judgment or rush to try to fix things apart from God's directives.

4. *Reaffirm God's promise of sustaining grace.* Say to the Lord, "I trust that You are with me, and that You will carry me through this ordeal to the glory of Your name and to my eternal benefit. I rely on Your strength and presence to get me through this time of trouble." You may find it helpful to look up and recite aloud verses of Scripture in which God promises to heal, deliver, restore, and reward His faithful people. You may also find it helpful to meet periodically with others who will encourage you to trust God as you move through your difficult circumstance to the good end that the Lord desires for you.

5. *Resist any temptation to sin or to deny God.* Such temptation is a direct satanic attack on your life. The Word of God states that you are to "resist" the enemy, and when you do so, he will flee from you (James 4:7).

6. *Begin to explore ways in which you might grow through this experience.* A godly counselor—a person who loves the Lord Jesus Christ, has a proven Bible-based faith, and is experienced in counseling people in your situation—may be helpful to you. Face up to areas of weakness in your life, and review what you might do to become stronger in these areas.

7. *Deal with your adversaries in a godly way.* Jesus taught, "Love your enemies, bless those who curse you, do good to those who

hate you, and pray for those who spitefully use you and persecute you, that you may be sons of your Father in heaven" (Matt. 5:44–45).

To love means to give. You cannot love others without giving to them. Give something positive to your enemies who may be trying to take something from you. Speak well of those who speak ill of you. Pray for those who are out to do you in. Recognize that those who do ill to you as a child of God are not *of* God; rather, they operate as Satan's messengers. They are doing Satan's work for him. You must hate Satan, not his messengers. When you treat your enemies with love, words of blessing, and prayer, you neutralize them. Satan no longer can work through them.

8. *Read passages in Scripture in which people encountered adversity.* Be encouraged by the way in which God brought them through their adversity with victory.

9. *Reflect on ways in which you might minister to others in your adversity.* Comfort others; help others; give to others. Turn yourself outward.

10. *Ask the Lord to give you courage as you stand strong in faith, give to others in need, and remain true to your relationship with Him.*

These ten steps are for advancing in your spiritual life. As you look back through them, you will readily see that you don't need adversity to grow in these ways. Adversity, it seems, serves as something of a crash course to compel you to grow in the Lord. God is in the process of building you, of creating you, of making you into one of His saints on the earth. Yield to that process. Rejoice that He is forming you into the very likeness of Christ Jesus.

Ultimately, your response to adversity, regardless of the source of its origin, is to say to your heavenly Father, "Have Your way in my life." Adversity brings you to your knees. While you are on your knees, may you acknowledge Jesus as Lord and humble yourself before the Father so He can do His good work in you.

- *Can you recall an experience in your life in which you allowed the Lord to work in you and through you so that you advanced in your spiritual walk and emerged stronger in the Lord after your time of trial?*

_____

_____

• *How did you feel as you yielded to the Lord's work in your life? What was difficult about it? What was joyful about it?*

_____

_____

• *What new insights do you have about how to advance in your relationship with God when times of anguish, heartache, or trouble arise?*

_____

_____

• *In what ways is the Lord challenging you today to grow spiritually?*

_____

_____

MY FINAL WORD TO YOU

Have you ever watched a sculptor at work? The sculptor does not chisel away at the marble or mold the clay in a haphazard way as if hoping that a figure will emerge from it. To the contrary! The sculptor has in mind from the outset what she is trying to create. Sculptors throughout history have been recorded as saying that they are trying to release the figure encased in the stone, or that they are merely removing the excess marble that has the image trapped within it.

How much more so in the case of the divine Sculptor, our heavenly Father. He uses adversity to chip away at things that have us in bondage to the enemy of our souls. He uses adversity to smooth the rough places in our lives. He uses adversity to break away the trivia in which we often imprison ourselves. And all the while, His purpose is to reveal the image of Christ Jesus within us so that we may be masterpieces of His creative and redemptive power to others who view our lives.

Even as we resist the enemy of our souls and shield ourselves against the painful blows of the chisel against our lives, we can also yield ourselves in spirit to the good work that the Father is producing in us. Any pain that we feel today will one day yield to the great joy of knowing that the Lord has fashioned us, and He is preparing us for greater use in His kingdom.

We must never lose sight of the fact that the Father does His sculpting work with love. It is *because* He loves us that He chastens us, disciplines us, and seeks our perfection. It is *because* of His love that He allowed Jesus to be crucified on a cross. That act of love, as painful and horrible as it was, brought about not only the glorification of Jesus, but also the possibility of redemption for all humanity. The Lord's act of love in allowing us to be crucified daily in Christ Jesus is for a similar purpose—to bring about our glorification as a reflection of the Lord at work today and to bring others to a saving knowledge of the Lord. As Jesus prayed, so must we pray, "Not my will, Lord, but Your will."

His will is that you become fully conformed to the image of Christ, fully transformed in the renewal of your mind, fully filled with the Holy Spirit, and fully alive forever and ever. What a good purpose He has for you if you will only choose to advance in your spiritual growth when adversity comes your way!